**305 LOST BUILDINGS OF CANADA**

# 305 LOST BUILDINGS of CANADA

**Raymond Biesinger & Alex Bozikovic**

Text copyright © 2022 by Alex Bozikovic.
Images copyright © 2022 by Raymond Biesinger.

All rights reserved. No part of this work may be reproduced or used in any form or by any means, electronic or mechanical, including photocopying, recording, or any retrieval system, without the prior written permission of the publisher or a licence from the Canadian Copyright Licensing Agency (Access Copyright). To contact Access Copyright, visit accesscopyright.ca or call 1-800-893-5777.

Edited by Jill Ainsley.
Page design by Julie Scriver.
Cover design by Raymond Biesinger with Julie Scriver.
Cover illustrations (front cover, clockwise from top right) The Citizen Building, Ottawa; Pantages Theatre, Vancouver; Le Forum de Montréal; Hub Cigar, Edmonton; Honest Ed's, Toronto; Cecil Hotel, Calgary; Shell Tower, Toronto; Malcolm & Souter Furniture Company, Hamilton; (back cover, top to bottom) Birks Building, Hamilton; The Pink Poodle, St. John's; Regent Theatre, Winnipeg.
Printed in Canada by Friesens.
10 9 8 7 6 5 4 3 2

Library and Archives Canada Cataloguing in Publication

Title: 305 lost buildings of Canada / Raymond Biesinger and Alex Bozikovic.
Other titles: Three hundred and five lost buildings of Canada
Names: Biesinger, Raymond, artist. | Bozikovic, Alex, author.
Identifiers: Canadiana (print) 20210289759 | Canadiana (ebook) 20210289791 | ISBN 9781773102368 (softcover) | ISBN 9781773102382 (EPUB)
Subjects: LCSH: Lost architecture—Canada—Pictorial works. | LCSH: Buildings—Canada—History—Pictorial works. | LCSH: Architecture—Canada—History—Pictorial works. | LCGFT: Illustrated works.
Classification: LCC NA740.5.L67 B54 2022 | DDC 720.971/022—dc23

Goose Lane Editions acknowledges the generous support of the Government of Canada, the Canada Council for the Arts, and the Government of New Brunswick.

Goose Lane Editions
500 Beaverbrook Court, Suite 330
Fredericton, New Brunswick
CANADA E3B 5X4
gooselane.com

Goose Lane Editions is located on the traditional unceded territory of the Wəlastəkwiyik whose ancestors along with the Mi'kmaq and Peskotomuhkati Nations signed Peace and Friendship Treaties with the British Crown in the 1700s.

For Elizabeth — **RB**

To LM, JB, and BB — **AB**

# CONTENTS

Introduction 9

Glossary 195

Acknowledgements 199

St. John's 11
NL
Charlottetown 34
Moncton 39
PE
Halifax 23
QC
NB
Quebec City 56
Fredericton 36
NS
Montréal 45
Saint John 41
ON
Ottawa 91
Sherbrooke 66
Sudbury 104
Kingston 82
Guelph 68
Peterborough 100
Sarnia 102
Oshawa 89
Windsor 17
Toronto 106
Hamilton 71
Kitchener 85
London 87

## INTRODUCTION

In Rome, generations of buildings have been constructed on top of their forebears. Layers of history are preserved in tiers of stone. You can find such physical remnants in Canada, too, if you know where to look. In Montréal, dig through the earth where the Pointe-Saint-Charles shoreline was extended with construction debris in the 1930s. In Regina, you might be able to find columns and pediment of an old Canadian Bank of Commerce building in a mall atrium. That structure started its life a century earlier on Winnipeg's Main Street. The old Bank of Toronto building at King and Bay Streets is long gone, but these days pieces of its stone columns rest at the Guild Inn, an hour's bike ride away.

Many more structures live on only in memory. Cities change. Buildings come and go. We all know this, and usually it's something we take for granted; another beat-up house, an empty church, an obsolete office building pulled down and sent off in dumpsters.

But we lose things along the way: traces of how we used to live, and the art and craft of previous generations. The movie theatre that was the centre of neighbourhood life; the letters that passed through Kelowna's unlikely art deco post office; the Cecil Hotel's rambling stories about Calgarian booms and busts.

This book uncovers some of those legacies. They're buildings from across the country that are now gone but still have something to say. Some are famous, such as Vancouver's Pantages Theatre, and preservationists have mourned their loss. Others went down without notice.

And, in a few places destruction was greeted as a gift. These are lost buildings that held certain people—Indigenous children, migrants, or young women who had given birth—and inflicted terrible suffering upon them. The world of heritage often overlooks the darker themes in our collective history. We have not.

Raymond is an illustrator and history enthusiast; Alex a critic who writes about buildings new and old. We've found stories to bring these structures to life, and studied old photographs, drawings, and records to recreate their details. Wherever possible, we have identified the architects and other designers. We have also identified what stands on the site of the building in 2021. Where no information is provided, the site is currently vacant.

Some of them are easy to love, with craftsmanship and detail that anyone could appreciate. Others speak a more subtle architectural language — including modernist buildings, products of an era when everything old could be thrown out that in turn fell victim to the same logic. And in some cases, architecture itself is irrelevant. No one paid attention to the building that housed Sam the Record Man in Toronto. It was the spinning records of neon on the front that were important. They became icons of a street and a city.

These are all places that mattered. The list is not definitive or exhaustive. Most of the buildings in this book have gone down in our lifetime. Others fell before we were born, in the great culling of buildings in the middle of the twentieth century.

Think of this book as an impossible architectural walking tour. It spans the country, its cities and countryside, and jumps across periods of history without hesitation.

We hope that after you've taken this city-by-city trip through what used to be here, you will think twice about how your home city is changing — or not changing. Heritage preservation is a complicated field, and it's never practical to hold onto every trace of the past. But what we ignore today, we may well see as treasure tomorrow. Buried treasure, perhaps, but still valuable.

## ST. JOHN'S, Newfoundland and Labrador

St. John's is perhaps the oldest city in Canada, and for most of its history it hasn't been Canadian. John Cabot probably landed in Newfoundland in 1497, but Portuguese, Spanish, and Basque ships all visited and fished for cod. When the city first showed up on a colonial map, it was as São João. The first permanent British settlement came in the 1630s, and the town was attacked by the Dutch and the French, who burned it. Not all the fires were acts of war; St. John's had a half-dozen accidental fires in the nineteenth century. Newfoundland argued over confederation for nearly a century, and in the interim the island gave many lives, and some of its strategic ground, to fight the two World Wars. The city's buildings reflect this stormy history (and the effects of actual storms, too, a big presence in local life). Much of the downtown was rebuilt after the Great Fire of 1892, including thousands of the saltbox houses that define the city's image. Legend has it this is when the tradition of painting houses in cheerful, contrasting colours began. In truth, the brightest colours date to the 1970s, a period when some locals overcame the forces of suburbanization and urban renewal to reclaim the old downtown. Much of the city's built heritage remains, but waves of commerce and politics (and fire) have taken away many places that linger in the minds of St. John'sers.

**Newfoundland Hotel** 1926-1983. Designed by Ross & Macdonald.

In the 1920s, Newfoundland's leaders believed the island needed a "modern" hotel to spur tourism. The Montréal firm T.E. Rousseau and the prominent Montréal architects Ross & Macdonald delivered a rather austere Edwardian classical, 168-room hotel with a double-height lobby and (very modern!) elevators. The hotel immediately ran into trouble, however, and the government was forced to take it over just as the Depression hit. When Newfoundland once again became a colony of Britain, the ceremony took place in the hotel's ballroom. And when Newfoundland struck a deal to join Confederation in 1947, it included the clause that the government of Canada would take control of this hotel. CN eventually managed it and demolished it to build a modern replacement for the 1980s. **Cavendish Square; now the parking lot for the Sheraton Hotel Newfoundland.**

**Newfoundland and Labrador**

## Star Theatre 1922-2010

This spot had a series of public halls from 1874 to 2010, serving purposes that included a courthouse, theatre venue, and movie house. The third building, constructed in 1922, was a theatre until 1957, when it was taken over by the Newfoundland Fishermen's Star of the Sea Association. The association (once the largest such fishermen's group) added a portico to the mansard-roofed shed of the building; after it was pulled down, only the name stuck.
**40 Henry Street; now Star of the Sea Residences.**

---

## New Hope Community Centre 1942-2015

In the early twentieth century, many of St. John's poor lived in crowded tenements in one central neighbourhood, which escaped the major fires of 1846 and 1892. The Salvation Army set up shop here as early as 1886 and took over a furniture factory on the edge of the so-called Central Slum. In 1942 it completed a replacement building: a three-storey hall with deco details constructed of poured concrete. This neighbourhood was emptied and razed, making way for private development and city hall. The New Hope Community Building made it to 2014, was damaged by a flood, and was replaced with a building that brings affordable housing back to the area.
**18 Springdale Street; now a new Salvation Army facility.**

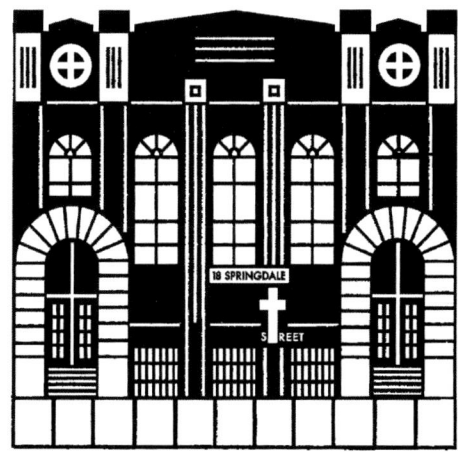

**Newfoundland and Labrador**

## Prince's Rink 1899-1941
Designed by Fred Angel and W.H. Murray.

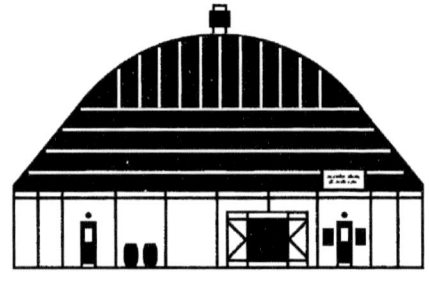

The rink was built on a railyard owned by Reid Newfoundland Company, whose railway connected the island's communities. The rink had a similar role as the leading venue for inter-community ice hockey games and, indeed, all winter sports in the capital. In 1937, the first artificial ice surface in Newfoundland was built under its barrel-vaulted wood roof. After the building burned, the province wouldn't get another artificial rink until 1954. **10 Fort William Place; now Baine Johnston Centre.**

---

## The Athenaeum 1878-1892
Designed by Sterling & Dewar with J. and J.T. Southcott.

Like many other working-class towns in the early nineteenth century, St. John's built a series of literary institutions, starting with a subscription library in 1810. Three such groups merged to create the Athenaeum; annual subscription, twenty shillings. This combined a library that held six thousand books with an auditorium. Its Second Empire-style building featured a high mansard roof and an elaborate front facade mixing stone arches and columns with complex corbelling and window tracery. The hall's ceiling featured paintings of Raphael, Shakespeare, Sir Walter Scott, and Edmund Burke—cultural icons of the day, larger than life. In 1886 an exhibition of a bull moose skull and antlers was greeted excitedly by the local newspaper. (Moose had not been introduced to the island.) The 1892 fire wiped out much of downtown, including the Athenaeum's building; the institution closed in 1898, leaving the city without a public library of any kind.
**285 Duckworth Street; now the former Provincial Museum.**

## General Post Office Building 1885-1950s

Newfoundland and Canada took control of their postal operations from British authorities in 1851. The Newfoundland Post Office constructed this assertive stone public building at the corner of Water and Queen Streets. Its architecture blended a sober neoclassicism with an oddly asymmetrical composition; the latter nods to the buildings David Ewart was designing for Canada's post offices at the time. In the 1950s, after Newfoundland joined Confederation, Canada Post replaced this with a new structure. A post office remains.

**354 Water Street; now a post office and private offices.**

---

## Octagon Hotel 1896-1915. Designed by Charles Danielle.

When he was nineteen years old, Charles Danielle opened a dancing school in Chicago, calling himself "a professor of the Terpsichorean art." A costume designer, dance teacher, hotelier, and restaurateur, "the professor" somehow ended up settling in Newfoundland not once but twice—the second time in the 1880s as promoter of fancy-dress balls and proprietor of Octagon Castle. Danielle designed and decorated this resort hotel with his own special flair: satin banners embroidered with silver and gold hung in the atrium, and upstairs a "mortuary room" housed a casket wrapped in embroidered black satin and velvet, ready for Danielle's end. He died in 1902 and was remembered, fifty years later, as "one of the most eccentric characters ever to set foot on Newfoundland."

**Topsail Road.**

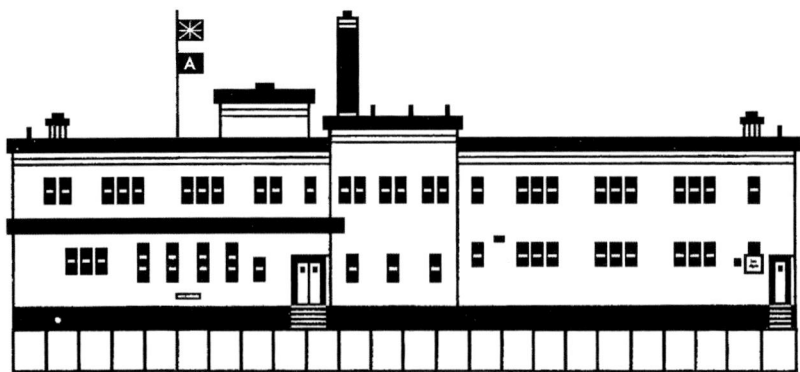

**Fort Pepperrell Air Force Base** 1941-2017

The British government gave the US Army the right to site a base in Newfoundland, and in 1940 the Americans chose a large site north of Quidi Vidi Lake. Construction was underway when Pearl Harbor brought the United States into the Second World War. Over five thousand American soldiers spent the war here, some of them manning anti-aircraft guns on Signal Hill. They withdrew in 1961, the Newfoundland and Canadian governments split the land, and the last American barracks—then belonging to the Canadian Forces—came down in 2017. **Charter Avenue.**

---

**The Pink Poodle** 1950s-1980s
Extension by Brown, Parsons, and Vivian, 1969.

In the mid-twentieth century, most of St. John's restaurants were diners. The Pink Poodle on Topsail Road was a favourite in Mount Pearl. One resident recalled years later that it was the upscale option, since you were given a knife and fork rather than just a toothpick in your sandwich. A 1969 addition to the building brought a kitschy neon sign. **675 Topsail Road; now a shopping plaza.**

## Ayre's Supermarket 1960-1998

The Ayre family took Newfoundland through two significant evolutions in retail, first founding a department store, Ayre & Sons, and then a chain of supermarkets as that type of food shopping took hold in the 1950s. But they soon sold their food stores to Dominion, reflecting the trend to fewer and bigger supermarket operators. This store lasted until 1994 as a Dominion and was demolished in 1998. **Elizabeth Avenue and Paton Street; now the Summerville Condominiums.**

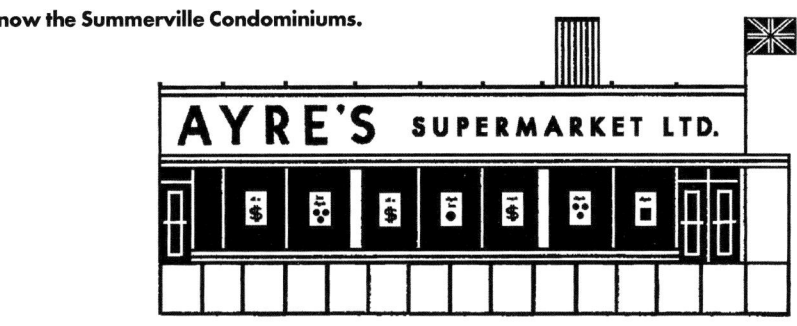

## Stone Chapel 1850s-1892. Designed by William R. Best.

The Congregational Church (an offshoot of Anglicanism) in St. John's dates back to 1775. It constructed this austerely Gothic structure with £1,200 collected from supporters in England. The Devon-born Best designed the building, and it was constructed by locals John Southcott and his son John T. Southcott, who would become prominent architects in St. John's. It was largely destroyed by the Great Fire of 1892; the congregation opened a new wooden church in 1895 and lasted forty more years. That building is now condos. **39 Queens Road.**

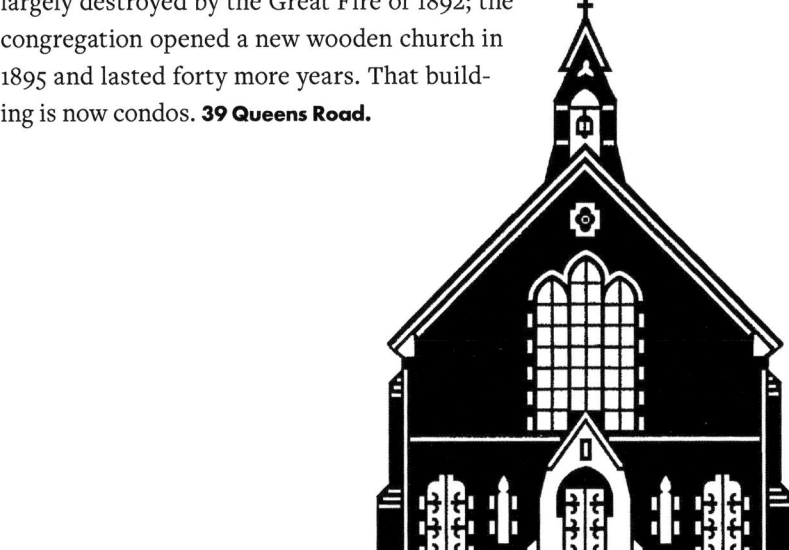

## Central Fire Hall
1895-1937

On July 8, 1892, a fire started in a St. John's stable. By the next day, nearly the entire city had burned, leaving eleven thousand people homeless. The fire department did not look good. Firefighters had emptied a large water-storage tank near the fire site and forgotten to refill it. The city was rebuilt, and control of the fire department passed from the city to the Newfoundland Constabulary. ("If this department is ever left again in the same hands," wrote a judge investigating the fire, "all I can say is that we deserve to be burnt.") This hall was part of the rebuilding process, with a five-storey tower that overlooked the entire town. By the 1930s it was found to be obsolete and was replaced with a concrete building, which has in turn been replaced. **5 Fort Townsend.**

---

## "Slum" House 1880s-1952

Many St. John'sers were displaced by the fire of 1846, and thousands settled here in what became known as the Central Slum, joined by more people after the even larger 1892 fire. (Colour photos suggest the houses here were not, in fact, brightly painted.) Local and Newfoundland governments bickered for half a century on what to do about the area, bringing in various town planners to reimagine the place but never finding enough resources. After Newfoundland joined Confederation, St. John's adopted federal policies of "slum clearance" and the accompanying funds, and constructed new social housing in the suburbs for the residents. **Central Street.**

## Garland's Shed 1880s-2010

Fishing is fundamental to the culture and economy of Newfoundland, and it can be a difficult and dangerous business, even here. The Battery, at the mouth of St. John's Harbour and the base of Signal Hill, has often been hit by rockfalls and avalanches over the years, to the peril of the fishers and families who live here. But in 2010, it was a winter storm that devastated the Outer Battery, taking with it all of Critch's Wharf and several buildings including the century-old family fishing hut of Keith Garland, which slid into the water. **Outer Battery Road.**

## Belvedere Orphanage 1885-2017. Designed by Bishop M.F. Howley.

When this building burned down, local built-heritage advocates were saddened by the loss; some women who had a history here were not. For its first eighty years, this four-storey Second Empire structure, apparently designed by the local bishop, housed an orphanage run by the Sisters of Mercy. Decades later, women who had grown up there recalled being brutally and repeatedly beaten by the nuns who raised them. Later the building became a school, and offices for the Roman Catholic School Board for St. John's. It sat vacant for years before a fire, for better and for worse, took most of it down. **Margaret's Place.**

**Holloway School** 1892-1984. Designed by A.C.P. Paine.

A Methodist school from 1860, this site was wiped out by the Great Fire of 1892, and Paine designed a new building that channelled the fashionable Richardsonian Romanesque style in rather austere form. Built up against a tall rock face, it had a door at the back that opened onto the top floor and one to the front two floors down; students wore down the stone of the steps while ascending and descending. In 1925, the interior burned, and Paine reconstructed it without a tower. After the school was closed in 1980 and sold to developers, its new owners proposed a new twelve-storey building, which prompted a long planning dispute and, in the end, no new building. The house's stone wall remains today. **99 Long's Hill; now a parking lot.**

## Waterford Manor

1905-2018. Designed by William Butler.

This was a mansion with many stories. Its architect, Butler, was a St. John's native who went away, including to Chicago to work on the 1893 World's Fair, and returned home to design some of the city's grandest houses. He created this one for Andrew Delgado, who owned a "candy and fruit emporium" on Water Street. (That building, also by Butler, still stands.) But the house passed into the hands of business and political leaders, first Sir Edgar R. Bowring and then Peter Cashin, before the government took it over for an orphanage and other uses. In 2018, it was a bed-and-breakfast when somebody burned it to the ground; a member of the family that owned the house was charged with arson but acquitted. **185 Waterford Bridge Road.**

---

## City Hall
1885-1971. Designed by George H. Jost.

The architect Jost lived in St. John's in the 1880s when he was working for Brookfield, a large Halifax construction company. While there, he designed this Fisherman's and Seaman's Home to provide lodging for men in those trades. But in 1911 the city government moved in, and the old structure—its Second Empire style apparently good enough for civic business—became the city hall for sixty years. The land is still in public hands; it's the heart of the city's entertainment district.
**387 Duckworth Street; now Prince Edward Plaza.**

**Newfoundland and Labrador**

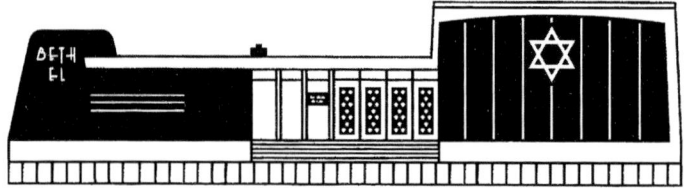

**Beth El Synagogue** 1956-2000. Designed by Cummings & Campbell.

The architect Angus "Angles" Campbell was a Newfoundlander, a largely self-taught architect, and a passionate modernist. He and his partner designed Newfoundland House, Joey Smallwood's 1959 country residence, and also the Bowring's department store. Here, for the only synagogue on the island, he employed a language of triangles and hexagons that evoked Frank Lloyd Wright and also the Star of David, the central symbol of Judaism. Another religious symbol, a Tree of Life, took shelter in the courtyard. In the late 1990s, the shrinking congregation downsized its facility. It demolished the synagogue's west wing and courtyard to see them replaced by an oversized house. **128 Elizabeth Avenue.**

---

### Grace General Hospital 1923-2008

The Grace opened in 1923 as a maternity hospital and grew into much more. Its building, whose gables and dormers gave it a slightly domestic feeling, expanded dramatically in the postwar period. Mary Southcott (her father was one of the architect Southcotts), an innovative leader of the nursing profession, helped create a nursing school here. The hospital shut down in 2000, and most of the buildings were demolished over the next few years, leaving only a modernist eight-storey nurses' residence, which has been empty for a decade. **Lemarchant Road.**

# HALIFAX, Nova Scotia

For 250 years, waves of building and rebuilding have passed over the city. The place the Mi'kmaq called K'jipuktuk (or Great Harbour) attracted the attention of French and British colonists. The British fortified the city in the mid-1700s, and it would have a significant naval presence for another 150 years. Ordnance literally reshaped the city through the Halifax Explosion of 1917, caused by a ship full of military high explosives. That disaster prompted much rebuilding. But other forces have been at work on the fabric of the city, not least the urban renewal of the mid-twentieth century. Ideas about the car, old buildings, and "blight" didn't wipe out downtown here, as they did in other cities, but they certainly made their mark, not least on the city's racialized and low-income residents. A city that values its history has, nevertheless, discarded many of its physical traces.

---

### Citadel Inn 1963-2012

It was close to Citadel Hall, but as a low-lying motel the Citadel Inn was uncontroversial. When the owner proposed an eleven-storey tower in 1971, however, that prompted a huge controversy. The resulting concrete tower spurred new policy that protects views to and from Citadel Hill. The building itself was once extremely chic, with an International Style white box balancing the heavier, asymmetrical concrete tower. The replacement hotel is taller but much less stylish. **1960 Brunswick Street; now a Hampton Inn.**

## Moir's Factory & Warehouse 1889-1975
Designed in part by Dumaresq & Cobb.

Once, downtown smelled like chocolate. Moir's was established in 1830 as a bakery but moved into chocolate in the 1870s. Over the next century it grew to make seventy-five kinds of packaged chocolate, including the Pot of Gold brand sold widely across the country. Its downtown factory complex sprawled across half a block, along Argyle from George to Duke. A water tower advertised Moir's "chocolate, bread and biscuits." Production moved across to Dartmouth in 1975. **1820 Argyle Street; now the Scotiabank Centre.**

## Capitol Theatre 1930-1974
Designed by Murray Brown.

The first colonial building on this site was Horseman's Fort, part of the defenses of Halifax enacted by Edward Cornwallis. By the 1870s it housed a large concert hall, which was replaced by this movie palace in the 1930s. The architect Brown, a theatre specialist, employed an "atmospheric" design for the lobby: the ceiling was lit to resemble a starry sky. Under the sky was the portcullis to a castle, and the theatre continued that theme with stone-look walls studded with turrets and pierced by stained glass. MT&T bought the building in 1973 and tore it down soon afterwards for its office-tower project. **1505 Barrington Street; now the Maritime Centre.**

## CBC Building

1933-2016

Designed by Sidney Perry Dumaresq.

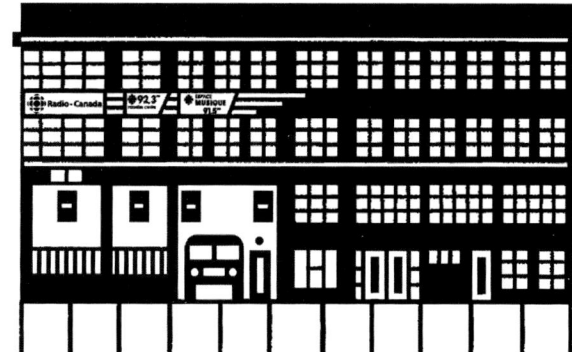

The local car dealer Fred Manning had a problem: how to fit a car dealership, offices, and parking onto a crowded downtown site? Dumaresq solved this by designing a Streamline Moderne building with a car elevator and parking on the roof. The building found a new purpose when the CBC took it over a decade later (keeping the elevator). Luckily the architect's novel choice of material, concrete, made the building well suited for a public organization that shared the latest news. **5640 Sackville Street; now Pavilion Condominiums and John W. Lindsay YMCA.**

---

## Dalhousie Medical and Dental Library 1937-1965

Designed by Sidney Perry Dumaresq.

After sixty years in lesser quarters, the medical and dental library moved into this purpose-built home in the late 1930s. With stone corbels and urns, it was a solidly classical structure for learning, with a hint of Arts and Crafts in its "tapestry brick." The Second World War broke out soon after the library opened, and the medical school found itself busily serving the war effort; the library was open evenings, weekends, and even through lunch. In the postwar years the Tupper Building, a centennial project, replaced the library.

**5850 College Street; now the Sir Charles Tupper Medical Building.**

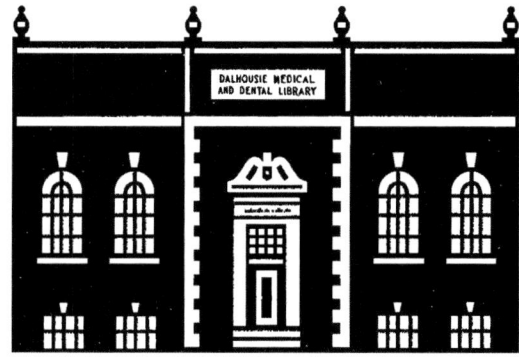

Nova Scotia

**City Market Building** 1913-1967. Designed by Sidney Perry Dumaresq.

The Halifax Farmers' Market was established in 1750 on Bedford Row, and it is the oldest continuously running market in North America. The market has operated in fourteen locations, including this high, gabled shed designed for it by the important local architect Dumaresq. By the 1950s public markets were fading in importance, and the police took over much of the structure, which was then demolished in the urban renewal fervour of the 1960s. **Now an apartment building at 1856 Albemarle Street.**

---

**Leon Steed's House** 1920s-1965

Some Black Haligonians founded a distinct community here on the very edge of the city, overlooking the Bedford Basin. This was home to about one hundred people, with a school, church, and shops, yet governments treated the area literally as a dumping ground and placed an infectious disease hospital nearby. The city never provided basic services. Amid all this, people lived in a close-knit, multi-generational community that included Leon Steed and his family. "We all live in our own homes out there, detached homes, where our children can run around," he said to a journalist in 1963. "We couldn't go and live in no apartments today—segregated or not segregated—discriminated [against] that we are." But the city targeted the "blight" of the area and expropriated the entire neighbourhood. By 1966 police had shot the Steeds' pet Pomerian, claiming it was a dangerous animal, and the family had been forced out, along with their neighbours.
**Now part of Africville Park.**

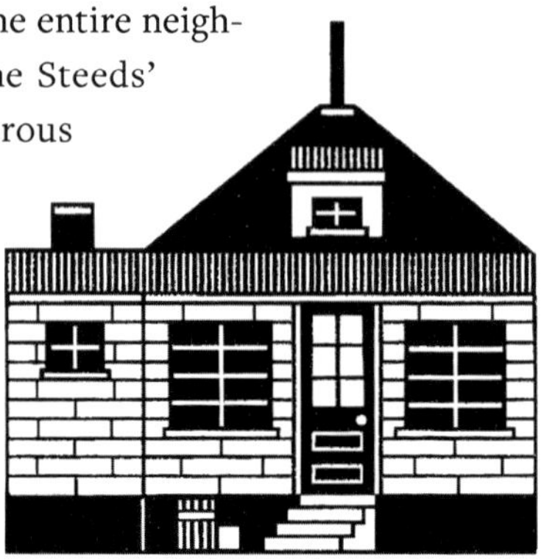

**Nova Scotia**

## Jost Mission 1871-1976

This church-like structure's architecture, with lancet-arched windows, echoed that of the nearby Brunswick Street Methodist Church. For most of a century, the mission provided a mix of religious and social services to working-class mothers and teens of the North End, eventually including a daycare, which still operates today in the suburbs. The institution was always effectively run by women: a "matron" or "deaconess" lived in the building. **1807 Brunswick Street. Now part of the the Scotiabank Centre.**

---

## The Trading Post 1850s-1967

In 1957, Halifax hired the British planner Gordon Stephenson to plan a modernization of the downtown. "The time is ripe for urban redevelopment and improvement, in which many of the bad results of nineteenth- and early twentieth-century vicissitudes may be removed," he wrote. This was Halifax's encounter with the postwar trend of urban renewal. Between 1958 and 1965, more than 2,500 buildings were demolished in the city. Most were houses; the residents, mostly low-income people, were displaced and often had nowhere immediately to go. Some of the lost buildings were found to be in dangerous condition; others in the way of planned highways and large-scale redevelopments such as Metro Centre (now Scotiabank Centre). This four-storey mansard-roofed Trading Post included apartments and a pawn shop that served the neighbourhood and port. The shop itself moved down to Granville and Duke into another nineteenth-century commercial building, which, in turn, was demolished, its facade folded into Barrington Place. **1854 Barrington Street. Now part of the the Scotiabank Centre.**

**St. Patrick's High School** 1953-2015. Designed by Downie, Baker & Ahern Architects-Engineers.

Catholic schooling in Halifax began in church basements, and by the mid-twentieth century was publicly funded on a large scale. Here, local architects designed a modernist concrete building whose forty-two classrooms, in keeping with the consensus in school design, had glass-block windows to allow in light while limiting distractions. Boys learned in the west wing; girls in the east. The building grew to 250,000 square feet and housed as many as 2,300 students before starting a long decline. It sat empty for a decade before the municipality tore it down. A redevelopment is in the works. **6067 Quinpool Road.**

---

### Sherbrooke Martello Tower
1827-1944

In the early nineteenth century, the British Royal Navy built a specific type of low, fortified tower across the empire. There were sixteen in Canada. (James Joyce once stayed in an Irish Martello tower, and the *Ulysses* protagonist Stephen Dedalus lives in one.) Soon after the War of 1812, the navy constructed this one at a military base on McNabs Island, thirty-three feet tall and fifty feet in diameter. Its outer skin was seven solid feet of brick and granite. Changes in artillery quickly made the Martellos obsolete, and this one was adapted into a lighthouse. During the Second World War, the ancient structure was replaced by a new lighthouse. **Now Maugher Beach Lighthouse.**

**Intercolonial Railway Station** 1877-1920. Designed by David Stirling.

This station and railway have an important role in Canadian Confederation: the promise of a railroad connecting Halifax to the other provinces helped John A. Macdonald convince the Maritime provinces to join. The federal government took over, renamed the Nova Scotia Railway, and built this impressive station, in the fashionable Second Empire style, as its terminus. The Halifax Explosion of December 1917 badly damaged the station, but it was quickly repaired. The ICR soon became CN, and the current Halifax Station supplanted this older one in the 1920s. **Barrington and North Streets; now the area beneath the Angus L. Macdonald Bridge.**

## Sweet Basil 1840s-2008

This was one of the last commercial buildings from Halifax's age of sail to remain standing. During its century and a half, it housed businesses from grocer to liquor store to tobacconist to restaurant. It was threatened by 1970s plans for an expressway, of which only the Cogswell Interchange was built. Thirty years later, the fronts of its neighbours were preserved as part of a new office-tower development; this one made way for the new building's front door, in a faux-historic facade.
**1866 Upper Water Street; now the RBC Waterside Centre.**

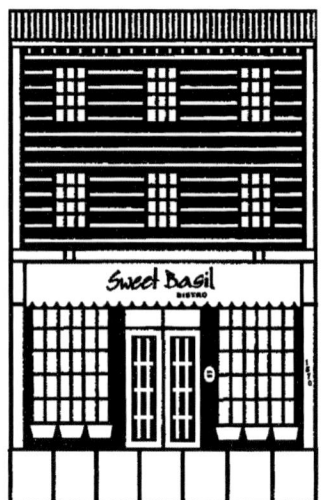

## Shannon Park 1950s-2017

In the nineteenth century, this plot of land facing Tufts Cove was a Mi'kmaq village called Turtle Grove. In the 1950s, the Royal Canadian Navy rebuilt it as a neighbourhood of modernist housing for navy personnel and their families. The project scattered forty-four three- and four-storey buildings in irregular fashion across a mostly green site, very much like the social housing then being built in British and Scandinavian suburbs (and, soon, in Canadian cities). Shannon Park was closed in 2004 and awaits redevelopment; the Canada 150 Trail and Lookout occupies part of the site.
**Off Sioux Road, Dartmouth.**

## Mills Brothers 1919-1966

This upscale clothing store anchored the shopping strip on Spring Garden for decades. When it burned in 1966, it occupied the ground floor of a three-building Victorian block with chic deco signage. The store was rebuilt and acquired a Tudor-style front. At Christmas, the old building housed a display of animatronic dolls that was famous within the city. The dolls were badly damaged in the 1966 fire but were restored and brought back in the 1970s. The Mills Brothers store finally closed in 2015 after nearly a century in operation; the existing building is turning into a mixed-use redevelopment.
**5485 Spring Garden Road.**

## Octagon House 1871-1969
Designed by Henry Elliot.

The Starr Manufacturing Company was among the world's leading manufacturers of ice skates; their Acme Spring Skate snapped onto your boot, ready in a moment to hit the ice. The company's prosperity paid off for factory manager Gavin Holliday. He commissioned himself a large house overlooking Sullivan's Pond that was octagonal, topped by an octagonal cupola. The architecture followed a trend pioneered by the American writer Orson Fowler, who wrote that an octagon is beautiful because it resembles a sphere, "the predominant or governing form of nature." Fowler was otherwise known for advancing the racist pseudoscience of phrenology, which analyzed the size and shape of a person's skull as an index to their psychology. **Crichton Avenue and Oak Street, Dartmouth; now the Oak Street Apartments.**

## Irving Arch 1890s-1982

Halifax's central waterfront was a place of industry right up until the late twentieth century. One of its major stocks in trade: oil. The *Halifax Herald* reported in 1917 that Halifax would become "the greatest oil distributing point on the North Atlantic coast." Irving arrived in 1937, taking over the former wharf of the Plant Steamship Company and building oil tanks. Plant, like its neighbours, had a building fronting squarely on busy Water Street, pierced by an arched passageway allowing access to a courtyard behind and then to the water. The Irving site was cleared in the 1980s, just as the Maritime Museum was built next door, another act in the transition of the port from industry to ice cream shops. **175 Lower Water Street at Sackville; now Sackville Landing.**

---

## Halifax Infants' Home 1899-2014. Designed by J.C. Dumaresq.

This home was built at a time when giving birth out of wedlock would bring profound stigma to a young woman — and for those without privilege, a dark future for mother and child. The alternative, in places like this, was a period of work and then usually giving up the child for adoption. Prominent architect Dumaresq designed a Second Empire building to house the institution, giving it a vaguely domestic character. And it would serve much the same purpose even into the 1990s, under the management of the Salvation Army. Saint Mary's University bought the building then and tore it down in 2014, obscuring its history, for worse or for better. **980 Tower Road.**

## African Methodist Episcopal Zion Church 1846-1955

There has been a sizeable community of Black Haligonians since the late eighteenth century, yet they were long segregated into a few specific neighbourhoods. One was here, along Gottingen Street in the then prosperous North End. In the years around 1900 this church, part of a Black-led branch of Methodism brought to Nova Scotia by Black Loyalists, stood at the community's centre, running a school and charitable work. The church's congregation shrank as other Black churches grew, but after 1930 the church was restored with community help—and then vandalized. Suburbanization and urban renewal programs decimated the neighbourhood's buildings, and the church was demolished in the 1950s. **26 Gottingen Street and Falkland Streets; now an empty lot.**

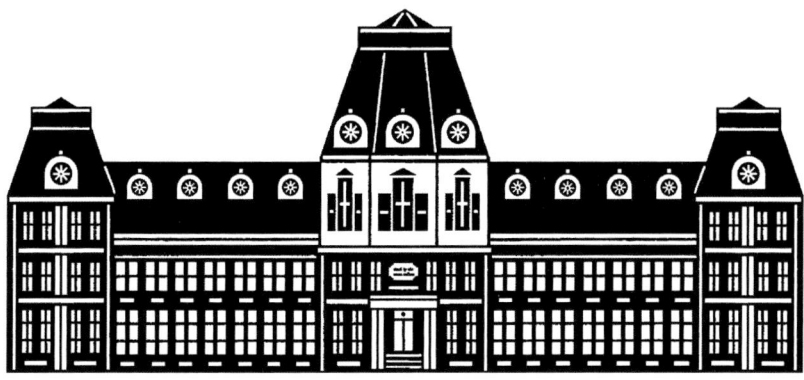

## Halifax Exhibition Building 1879-1907. Designed by Edward Keating.

Canadian cities built many grand exhibition buildings in the Victorian era, and this was among the grandest. Keating, then the city's chief architect, created six different versions of the design. He settled on a 261-foot-long arch-topped hall punctuated by three towers with cupolas. The hall, whose modern engineering allowed for a surprising number of windows, was used for exhibitions in summer and a skating rink in winter. The building was moved (minus its towers) to South Street in 1907 to serve as a skating rink. Its replacement, the new exhibition building, was destroyed in the 1917 Halifax explosion. **Near Victoria Park; now Cathedral Church of All Saints.**

# CHARLOTTETOWN, Prince Edward Island

The Charlottetown area was first settled by the French, and in 1758 the British expelled the remaining Acadians, built Fort Amherst, imposed a typical gridiron plan, and named the place after Queen Charlotte. They imported the fashion for Palladian neoclassicism and a veneration of stone buildings; though wood was the obvious building material here, it was occasionally painted to look like stone. Charlottetown was quiet enough in the twentieth century to keep much of what it had, though cars and suburbanization did change the place. The creation of Confederation Centre of the Arts cost the city some of its historic heart.

---

### The Cabot Building
1887-1963
Designed by David Stirling & William C. Harris.

Charles Morris's plan for Charlottetown put Queen Square at its heart. The city's first market building stood in the middle, where Province House is today, before being moved 294 feet northwest to the newly named Market Square. Nearby, the Cabot Building stood next to Province House, a red-brick structure that was less classical and more eclectic than its serious neighbour. A series of fires hit the area in the nineteenth and twentieth centuries, consuming a series of market buildings. The Cabot Building, however, was deliberately demolished for a new landmark.
**Richmond Street; now Confederation Centre for the Arts.**

**Prince Edward Island**

### Peter Pan Drive-In 1958-2020

In the postwar years, the Peter Pan was beloved by locals for its milkshakes, burgers (served in a basket), and lobster burgers. There were few franchised fast-food restaurants at the time; this locally owned place in an A-frame building was a landmark. The restaurant closed in 2013 and was demolished, but carpenters from Holland College rescued its sign, featuring Peter Pan and lettering that seemed to have been created by a young child.

**711 University Avenue; demolished.**

### Charlottetown Public Library

1930-1962

Designed by James Harris.

Facing Grafton Street and Market Square, this was the city's first public library, a sandstone Beaux-Arts pile whose architecture connoted classical learning. Its upper floor held a gallery devoted to the paintings of Robert Harris, whose nephew designed the building. (Robert's brother William was an architect of the Cabot Building.) In 1934 it was renovated when the Carnegie Foundation chose PEI for a community library demonstration project, which came with four thousand additional books. At the same time, a librarian toured the province in a bookmobile she had fashioned from a Chevy coupe.

**Now part of Confederation Centre for the Arts.**

## FREDERICTON, New Brunswick

New Brunswick's capital has seen centuries of construction and erasure. The Wəlastəkwiyik farmed this area, and the French built Fort Nashwaak, which served as the capital of Acadia. But British rule wiped out most physical evidence of Indigenous presence and Acadian settlement. The city grew in a sustained way with the arrival of Second Empire Loyalists and Fredericton's choice as the provincial capital in 1785. These changes brought some restrained New England architecture and then some showy public buildings, including the 1882 legislature and the 1876 city hall. (Next to city hall, the courthouse's lancet-arched front doors are a trace of a Victorian-era normal school that burned down.) What was lost along the way fell to fire, to age, and to twentieth-century changes in taste that rendered even well-made public buildings dispensable.

---

### The Risteen Building
1820s-2019

Early colonial New Brunswick was not a wealthy place, and most houses were made of local wood. Anthony Lockwood, the province's surveyor general, built this one out of cut stone in the early 1820s. Soon thereafter, he tried—by himself—to overthrow the colonial government and was shipped to Britain a prisoner. The house lasted until an 1870 fire, after which it was rebuilt as the Risteen Sash and Door Factory. This sensible wood-building enterprise lasted until the 1970s. The structure was demolished as part of a redevelopment project. **102 Queen Street; demolished.**

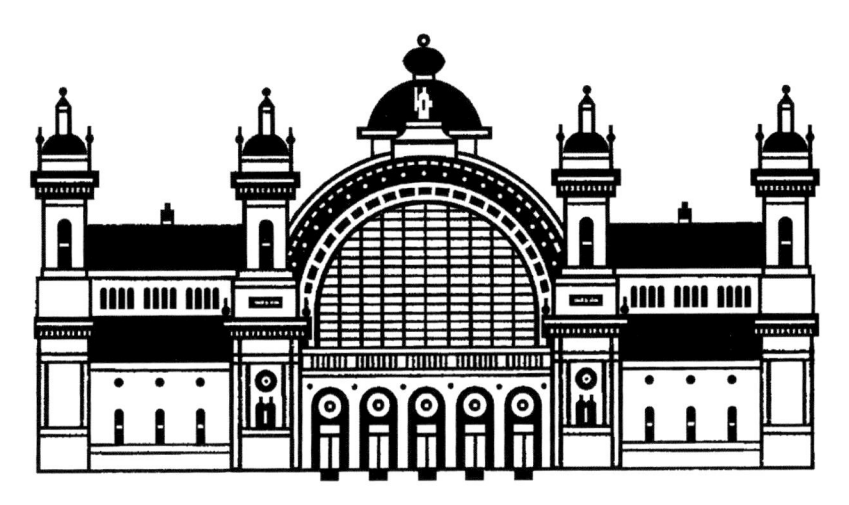

**Exhibition Palace** 1864-1877. Designed by Matthew Stead.

After London's Great Exhibition of 1851, agricultural and technological exhibitions spread across Canada. A decade later, the architect Stead designed this skyscraping structure with a $28,000 budget. His design arranged four wings in the shape of a cross, each ending in a large semi-circular window and a pair of turrets. (This looked rather like a railway station, the railway itself a powerful sign of progress.) A journalist reported the interior was "as light and gay as colours can make it." Evening illumination came from 650 gas-burning fixtures; great winged dragons spat flame.
**Westmorland and Saunders Streets.**

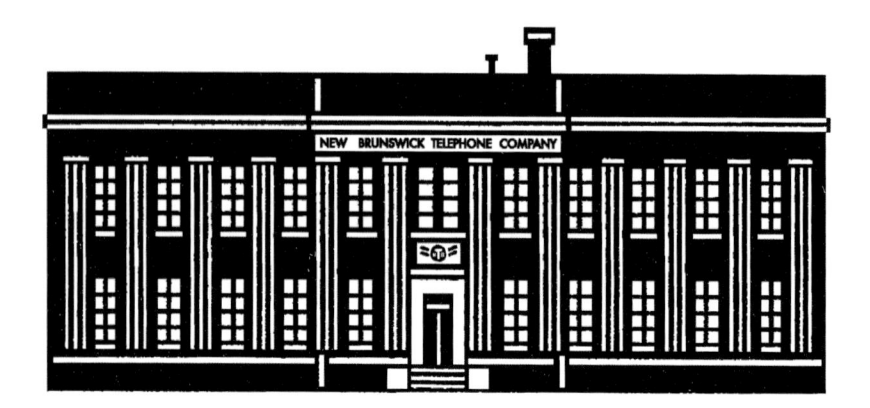

## New Brunswick Telephone Company Dial Exchange Building 1949-1990. Designed by Alward & Gillies and H. Claire Mott.

The province's telephone company, like many big Canadian institutions, was conservative in its architectural taste. For this two-storey building on King Street, a team of Saint John architects used the style now known as modern classical or stripped classical. The sandstone front featured twelve pilasters, ornamental rectilinear columns that were almost two-dimensional. The building looked back to classical tradition and forward to a modern world, depicted in the stone carving of telephone lines above the front door. **551 King Street; now a commercial building.**

## MONCTON, New Brunswick

Moncton is a city in which much has been lost. The site was a Mi'kmaq village, of which no trace remains. Acadians settled here in the 1670s; during the Expulsion after 1755, the British burned most of what they had built. The town then known as the Bend was small and quiet. It became a waypoint from Halifax to Saint John, a shipbuilding centre, and, rather quickly, a city. When the Intercolonial Railway placed its headquarters here in 1871, it transformed Moncton's fortunes. There have been ups and downs since then: the resurgence of Acadian arts and letters, the vanishing of the railways, and changes in taste and habits that erased an artful church.

---

**Saint Louis-de-France Church** 1972-2019. Designed by Gerry Gaudet.

Across Canada, major public buildings of the 1960s and 1970s share the brutalist style, as do a few Catholic churches, symbols of a period of intellectual openness within that church. New Brunswick got two, and this one was a fine example of the idiom: basically a cube, but rotated at an angle, its walls striated by diagonal lines of the formwork that created it. (Two bulbous ocular windows earned it the nickname "the frog church.") In 1975, the architect and sculptor Arcade Albert added a bell tower and crucifix. A declining congregation led to the closing of the church and its demolition.
**5 Pleasant Street; now an apartment building.**

## Intercolonial Railway General Offices 1880-1882

The Intercolonial Railway linked the Maritimes with Quebec, running from Halifax to Montréal without crossing into the United States, and its hub was here in Moncton. This gave the city a major economic boost, both with jobs on the railway and for the industry that grew up around it. Its headquarters, a stolidly Georgian neoclassical pile with ungainly stone quoining, was probably designed by the ICR's staff of engineers and architects. It burned in 1882. The Intercolonial later became part of CN, which remained a major employer in Moncton until 1988.

**Near Vaughan Harvey Boulevard and Main Street.**

---

## Moncton Sugar Company
1879-1896

John Leonard Harris remade Moncton. He and his brother Christopher were well-connected and affluent, but unlike many of their peers they were willing to take some entrepreneurial risk. John Harris led the creation of Moncton's first gasworks and water system, developed large areas of the town, and led its town council for a time. The Harris interests included ships—a crucial part of the local economy—and, for a time, sugar. The refinery was started in 1879 and running by 1881. One of its towers was eight storeys tall, and it dominated the skyline, a symbol of the newly industrialized city. Ships arrived from the West Indies carrying the raw materials, up to three hundred workers processed them, and the refined sugar left by rail. The building was destroyed by fire in 1896, but the Harrises were on to other things, and it was not rebuilt.

**Northeast corner of King Street and Main Street.**

**New Brunswick**

# SAINT JOHN, New Brunswick

A port city from the start, Saint John has been remade by tides of trade and migration. So have its buildings. American Loyalists brought an architectural language that informed Saint John houses. A major fire in 1877 wiped out much of the place, clearing the way for a wave of fine stone and brick buildings. The city's Black community grew to prominence and then shrank. Great public institutions were built, and then wiped out by the car and suburbanization. Saint John has retained more of its built heritage than many other places, but it has lost some.

---

## Jellybean Houses 1860s-2017

These brightly painted Second Empire houses were typical in the Saint John of the 1860s and 1870s, but most of their peers burned in the Great Fire of 1877, which consumed three-quarters of the city. These two houses were also the site of the first lending library in Saint John. In 2008 the city purchased the houses but failed to find a buyer. Over years of vacancy, they deteriorated and were demolished. Now, Saint John Non-Profit Housing is building a replacement, which may not be brightly coloured but will house dozens of people and likely a restaurant.

**15 and 19 Wellington Row.**

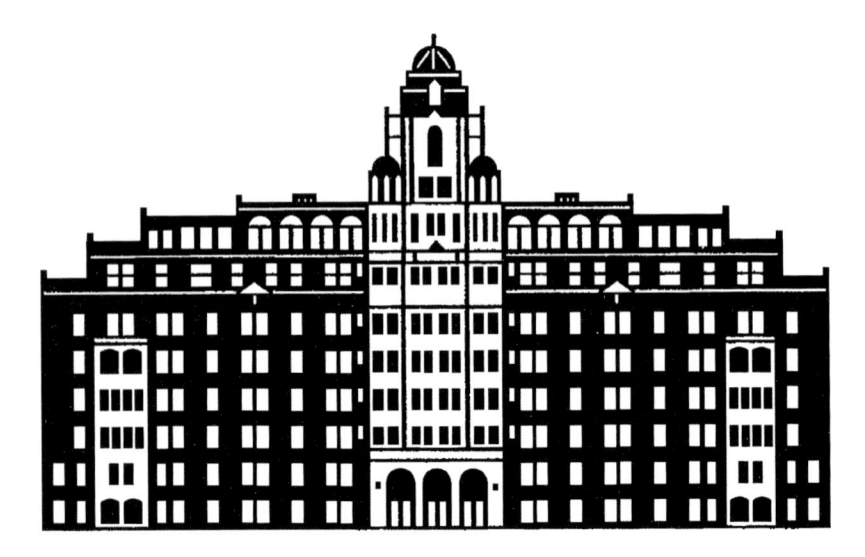

**Saint John General Hospital** 1931-1995
Designed by Pond, Pond, Martin & Lloyd with Alward & Gillies.

Completed in the depths of the Depression, this three-winged art deco hospital was one of the tallest buildings in the Maritimes. Perched atop "Hospital Hill," its 140-foot-tall tower and cupola could be seen for miles. Starting in the 1970s, the province consolidated the local hospitals. In 1982, the hospital's final 214 patients were transferred in special trucks to the new hospital in Millidgeville. The original hospital building served as the athletes' village for the 1985 Canada Games, and then sat empty until it was imploded in 1995. The building's copper dome survived demolition and now rests in a local park. **Hospital Street, now known as Agar Place.**

## Gothic Arches Church 1882-2019
Designed by John Welch.

After the devastating fire of 1877, it was unclear how the city would rebuild itself. The Centenary Methodist Church, whose building on a hilltop site had burned, went big. They hired Welch, a Scottish Brooklynite who specialized in churches, to create the biggest Protestant church in town with space for two thousand. The Gothic Revival building had ornate (and fireproof) stonework, while the structure was crafted from huge logs of pine. The congregation moved out in 1999, and this became a concert venue known as the Gothic Arches. But after that closed, the building sat empty and fell into disrepair. The arches fell in 2019. **95 Wentworth Street; future site of an apartment building.**

---

## St. Philip's African Methodist Episcopal Church 1870s-1942

The AME Church was long the centre of Black life in Saint John. This congregation, established in 1859, came together for worship, schooling, and social gatherings in an era when Black New Brunswickers were relegated to separate sections in churches and were often barred from attending local schools. In 1916, the church led community protests against the showing of the film *Birth of a Nation* in the city; the province allowed it to be shown uncensored. The church building was demolished in 1942 after the congregation moved to a new, larger one, itself now gone. **Queen and Pitt Streets.**

**New Brunswick**

**Union Depot** 1884-1930. Designed by J.T.C McKean.

Passenger rail came downtown in the late nineteenth century via the Portland Valley, essentially on the route of today's Saint John Throughway. The Intercolonial Railway built this station on land reclaimed from a tidal basin. At the time, Portland and Saint John were separate towns; they didn't come together until 1889. The architect McKean employed the eclectic Second Empire style, which he had also employed at Fredericton's city hall. The station was replaced, and then the trains vanished altogether.
**Station Street; now Harbour Station.**

## MONTRÉAL, Quebec

Just as the St. Lawrence River rolls past Montréal, people and trade of all kinds have been moving through here for millennia. By the time Jacques Cartier visited here in 1535, the Iroquoians had already established the permanent settlement of Hochelaga. The island had no permanent bridges until 1930, but migration into the city linked Montréal not just to its colonial powers of France and Britain but also to the shtetls of Eastern Europe. Its buildings have seen fast-moving waves of change shaped by migration and money and violent Toryism. Successive layers of religious structures Catholic and Jewish, governments provincial and federal, commercial and fantastical, have made way for the new.

### Rockhead's Paradise 1931-1983

Rufus Rockhead would greet you personally as you reached the top of the steps to his nightclub, welcoming you into a world where the best jazz and swing musicians played with a Black house band. This was the neighbourhood where Oliver Jones and Oscar Peterson grew up; they, like other local musicians, honed their skills here in a place that was also a rare refuge for Black Montréalers and visitors.

**1258, rue Saint-Antoine Ouest;
now Tour des Canadiens 3.**

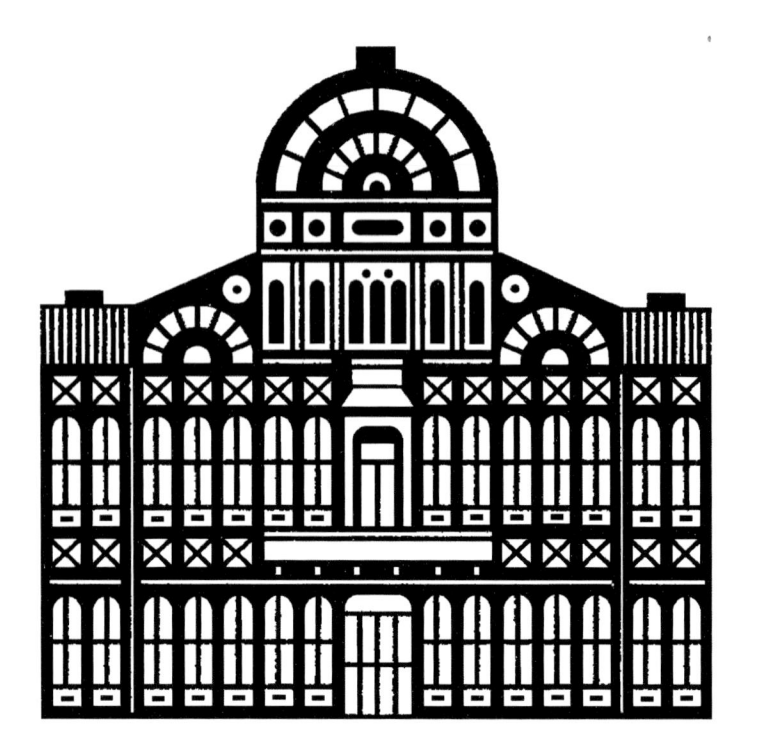

**Le Palais de Cristal** 1860-1896. Designed by John William Hopkins.

Named after the Crystal Palace at London's 1851 Great Exhibition, this hall was constructed on rue Sainte-Catherine for the Industrial Exhibition of 1860. The Montréal Board of Arts and Manufacture meant to make it permanent and so chose a solid material for its base: white brick with pink accents. The structure was moved to the Dominion Exhibition Ground (now Parc Jeanne-Mance) in the 1870s. Later, it housed one of the first indoor hockey rinks in Canada; the first recorded game was in 1875. In 1896, it, like many of its fellow crystal palaces, burned. **Parc Jeanne-Mance.**

**Palais du Commerce** 1952-2004. Designed by Roméo Desjardins.

The sign above the door read COMMERCE, and that was what this place offered—for a while. A series of Catholic institutions occupied this block for 150 years, including a reform school. As they left, the area by now called the Latin Quarter needed a new purpose, and a group of local entrepreneurs built this as an exhibition hall for commercial wares, like Chicago's Merchandise Mart. The new Place Bonaventure made it obsolete. The giant Palais housed an event space and skate park and the largest used bookstore in Montréal before, in an end to commerce, the Grande Bibliothèque du Québec replaced it. **475, boulevard De Maisonneuve Est.**

## Bonaventure Station

1887-1952. Designed by E.P. Hannaford with T.S. Scott.

When the Grand Trunk Railroad took over this terminal in 1864, it cleared the site and went big. GTR chief architect Hannaford designed a prestige piece for the railway, with mansard-roofed towers and Art Nouveau ornamentation on the stone facades and wood interior walls. After a fire largely destroyed the place in 1916, it was rebuilt with a flat roof. It lost most of its traffic in 1942 with the opening of Central Station; soon after another fire in 1948, it was wrecked.
**Now Chaboillez Square.**

**Queen's Hotel** 1893-1988. Designed by A.F. Dunlop.

This sandstone citadel stood near Windsor Station and Bonaventure Station. Its restaurants and bars welcomed middle-class travellers and locals both anglophone and francophone, including servicemembers during the First and Second World Wars. Things slowed down when Bonaventure Station closed in 1948, and this building, originally advertised as "a modern fireproof hotel," became an abandoned hulk between the highways and skyscrapers of the rebuilt downtown. Most of the structure was demolished in 1988; a wrecking ball felled the last bits of masonry in 1995. **Corner of rue Peel and rue Saint-Jacques; now a parking lot.**

## Architects' Building 1931-1968. Designed by Ross & Macdonald.

This deco tower, with terraces up to the seventeenth floor, housed architects, engineers, and others in the building industry. Ross & Macdonald, the important local firm who designed the structure, worked from the thirteenth floor. Naturally the building used the latest technology. Underground was a twenty-four-hour garage service for automobiles; a complex steel structure allowed large windows on all sides of all floors. But this artistry was hidden by sparingly oriented facades of Rockwood limestone, and the lobby was panelled in Notre Dame marble with brass accents. The structure closely resembled the 1931 Price Buiding in Quebec City, which survives; the Architects' Building was sold and demolished. **1135, côte du Beaver Hall; now a parking lot and a park.**

---

## Blue Bird Cafe 1930s-1972

It was a Friday night in downtown Montréal, and the Blue Bird was busy. So was the country bar upstairs, the Wagon Wheel, where Don & Curly & the Dudes were playing as usual. Then the Wagon Wheel bouncer turned away three drunken young men from the door. They returned with a can of gasoline and set fire to the stairs. Upstairs, an exit was blocked, and while many people escaped, thirty-seven were killed.
**1180, avenue Union; now apartments.**

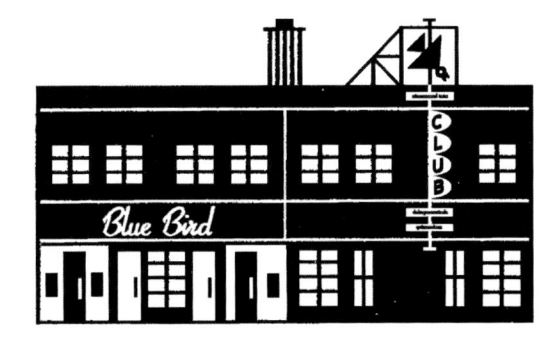

## Unitarian Church of the Messiah 1908-1987

Designed by Edward & W.S. Maxwell.

This church's Tudor-Gothic facade presented a sober aspect on rue Sherbrooke. Two towers of buff Indiana limestone framed a set of stained-glass windows, containing religious fervour within an architecture that fit the Golden Square Mile. The church moved here as its congregants flocked to the newly fashionable neighbourhood, and it outlasted many of them. But in 1987, the church's organist, Wilhelmina Tiemersma, set fire to the building in an attempted suicide; the blaze killed two firefighters instead. Tiemersma was convicted and served two years in prison. The church rebuilt in another location, bringing ornamental panels and stained glass from the old structure.
**1491, rue Sherbrooke at rue Simpson; now a residential building.**

---

## Laurier Palace Theatre
1912-1927

This large neighbourhood theatre held one thousand people, and it was a place of joy—until one night in 1927, when a small fire started in the theatre while 250 children were sitting in the balcony. The crowd of kids panicked and rushed for the exits, where many were trapped against the doors, which swung inward. Seventy-eight died; their funeral procession drew more than fifty thousand people. The fire prompted the creation of new rules requiring more circulation space, regulations that theatre doors always open outwards, and laws barring unaccompanied children under sixteen from theatres. That law lasted forty years, longer than the Laurier Palace itself. **3215, rue Sainte-Catherine Est; now a church.**

Quebec

## L'édifice Robillard 1879-2016
Designed by Daoust & Gendron.

Built of Montréal greystone, this four-storey structure mixed fashionable Romanesque with Byzantine flourishes, reflecting the growing wealth of the city's francophone middle class. By 1891 it was the Gaiety Museum and Theatorium, housing a wax museum and variety show. Soon afterward it became a vaudeville theatre, and in 1896 the first motion picture projection in Canada took place here: a set of short films by the Lumière brothers, projected on a screen the size of a towel. Through the twentieth century it housed all sorts of retailers out front and live music inside. It was being renovated when it caught fire in 2016. A similar building by the same architects still stands at 1076 boulevard Saint-Laurent. **974, boulevard Saint-Laurent; now a construction site.**

---

## Indians of Canada Pavilion, Expo 67 1967-1981
Designed by J.W. Francis.

The "Indians of Canada" got their own building at Expo, alongside those of European states and the United Nations. The pavilion's White architect chose its modernist-teepee form, but Indigenous artists, writers, and leaders had a strong influence over what was inside. Texts within the pavilion included propagandistic messages from the federal government but also spoke critically of forced assimilation and Christianization. Indigenous artists such as Norval Morrisseau contributed their work; Alex Janvier created a mural that was stubbornly abstract in style. The radicalism and tension of the pavilion faded, and the building itself was wrecked. **Île Notre-Dame; demolished.**

**Quebec**

## Le Spectrum 1952-2008

Behind the marquee was magic. This venue opened originally in 1952 as L'Alouette, and it became Le Spectrum in 1982, beginning an era in which this somewhat beat-up room hosted top touring acts on their way up, such as Radiohead, and locals like Martha Wainwright and The Dears. Stars would sometimes choose to play multiple nights here, as Jean Leloup did in 2000, rather than an arena show. The strings of light bulbs along the walls went dark in 2007. **318, rue Sainte-Catherine Ouest; now a shopping mall, tower, and parking lot.**

## Le Forum de Montréal 1925-1998. Designed by John Smith Archibald.

Hockey's holy place, this was the home of the Montréal Maroons and then, for seventy-one years, les Habs. Built for about 12,000 people—most in standing room—the arena was enlarged twice, and routinely sold out during more than thirty Stanley Cup final series up to 1993. Twenty-four cup banners hung from the rafters. Its architecture changed over the years. What began as a brick-and-steel structure lined with storefronts was largely rebuilt in the sixties. After the final game in 1996 (the home team won, and paid tribute to Maurice Richard), the Forum was gutted and became a theatre and party venue. **2313, rue Sainte-Catherine Ouest at avenue Atwater.**

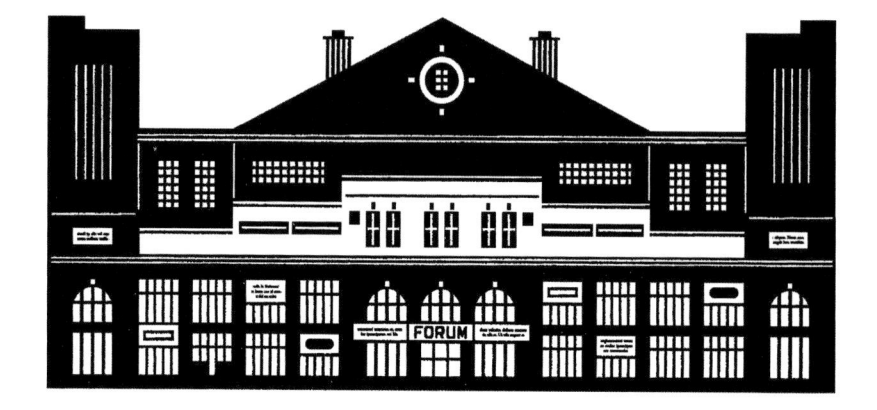

**Quebec**

## St. Ann's Market 1832-1849
Designed by John Wells & John Thompson.

This was a market, then a parliament. A two-storey neoclassical market building bridged the canalized Petite rivière Saint-Pierre, whose rushing waters helped keep the place cool and carried away garbage from the market. In 1842, the United Province of Canada decided to move parliament from Kingston, and the market building was renovated to hold the assembly, the legislative council, an archive, and a library with twenty-five thousand volumes. In 1851, a Tory mob burned the building down, and this was the end of Montréal's place as the capital of Canada. A new market was built in 1851 but demolished in 1901. **Now place d'Youville.**

---

## Silo No. 1 1902-1983

The first of Montréal's huge dockside grain elevators proved the city's importance as a grain-handling port, connecting the Prairies to the sea. It also represented twentieth-century engineering and technology—a tall concrete structure that stood over the old city like a monolith. In 1923, the leading modernist architect Le Corbusier published a photograph of a grain silo at the Port of Montréal, calling such buildings "the magnificent fruits of the new age." However, the 1970s construction of the new port created a different future for the old port as a place for leisure; this and some other silos were, with great difficulty, brought down.
**116, rue de la Commune.**

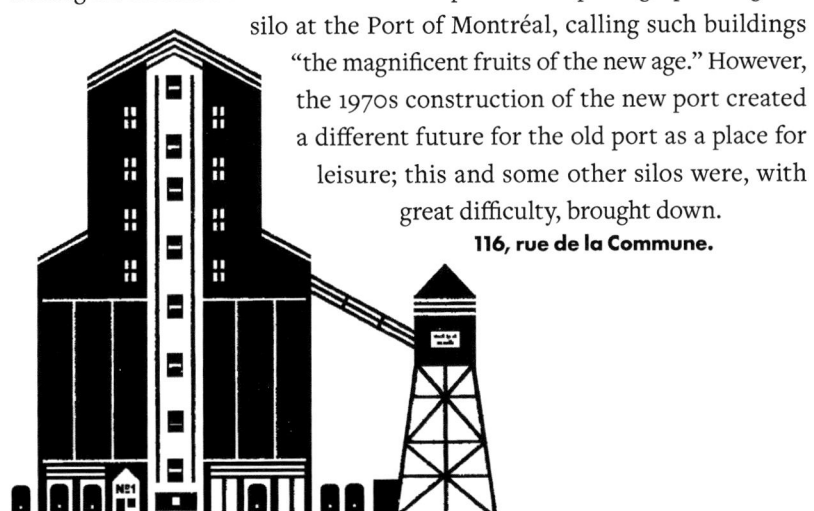

## Ben's De Luxe Delicatessen & Restaurant
1950-2008
Designed by Charles Davis Goodman.

In 1908, Benjamin Kravitz and Fanny Schwartz started serving smoked-meat sandwiches to fellow members of the Jewish community. Ben's soon became an institution, and the Kravitzes would, more than forty years later, hire the prominent local architect Goodman to design a moderne home for the deli, with coved lighting and terrazzo floors. At its peak in 1960, its servers (in white shirts and black bow ties) helped eight thousand customers per day. It was a regular stop for celebrities and, open twenty-two hours a day, a centre of the city's nightlife. It finally closed in 2006, and its decor went to the McCord Museum.

**990, boulevard de Maisonneuve Ouest; now Hotel Saint-Martin.**

---

## B'nai Jacob Synagogue 1902-1950s. Designed by Eric Mann.

In the 1880s, Montréal had a small, established Jewish community, concentrated in what is now Chinatown. This changed fast: a wave of Eastern European Jewish immigrants quickly transformed the community and the city. The new B'nai Jacob congregation in 1886 took over a downtown building from the older Shaar Hashomayim, who moved to the Golden Square Mile; B'nai Jacob reconstructed the building with some Byzantine stonework, common to synagogues of the time. Its five hundred seats were packed on the High Holy Days, and any other day of the year it was busy enough with Jews coming to pray, meet, and schmooze.

**970, rue de Bullion; now a vacant lot.**

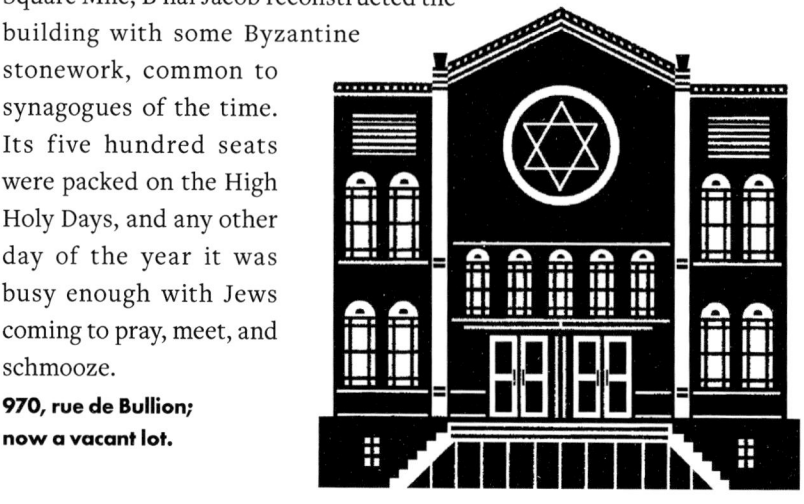

Quebec

## Redpath Mansion 1886-2014
Designed by Sir Andrew Taylor.

Naturally the Redpath family would settle here, in the Golden Square Mile neighbourhood. From 1870 to 1900, 70 per cent of Canada's wealth was held by residents of the area, not least the Redpaths, who founded the sugar refinery and built the Lachine Canal. Starting in the 1930s, the Redpaths and their peers left the neighbourhood, which became more commercial, but this red-brick-and-stone Queen Anne house lasted—sort of. It was partially demolished in 1986 before Heritage Montréal and Save Montréal succeeded in obtaining an injunction, and it was left in pieces, half-demolished and home to squatters, until 2014. **3457, avenue du Musée.**

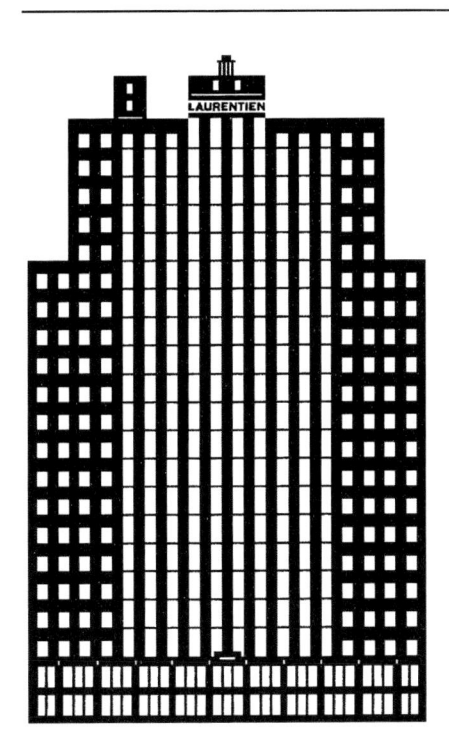

---

## Hotel Laurentien 1948-1978
Designed by Charles Davis Goodman.

A mountain on Dorchester Square, this midmarket hotel had one thousand rooms and stood twenty-three storeys tall. Local architect Goodman designed it in the Streamline Moderne style with wedding-cake setbacks and curved corners at the street; newspaper articles described it as a mainstay of budget tourism. By the early seventies, however, owner CP Rail saw a gold mine in the downtown's then booming office market. A CP official reassured Montréalers that the replacement would not be "stark" or "indifferent to human scale." The eventual 1980s result, however, was a Late Modernist mirror-glass office tower. **1100, boulevard René-Lévesque Ouest; now the La Laurentienne building.**

**Quebec**

# QUEBEC CITY, Quebec

Even in a city whose history has been well preserved, things pass. The current city was once the site of an Iroquoian town called Stadacona. After Samuel de Champlain colonized the area in 1608, the city grew quickly as a port for the fur trade. The people of New France used the local greystone to build fortifications and houses based on the architecture of their ancestral homes. What changed? The British conquest of the city in 1759 introduced some modest English influences into its architecture, but much of the early city remained untouched. Bustling Montréal overtook Quebec City economically, blunting the blades of development and redevelopment. Incremental change has taken away some important places—an innovative hospital wing, a public market, and exhibition buildings—but often it was fire that took away the city's built heritage, and many institutions remain where they were, their past architecture lingering in the collective memory like phantom limbs.

---

### La Maison Arnoux 1674-1893

Built in 1674 for Charles Palantin on the city's most prestigious street, this high-gabled, very French house became famous for a later visitor. The Marquis Louis-Joseph de Montcalm, badly wounded in the Battle of the Plains of Abraham, came here to seek aid from surgeon-major André Arnoux. Here Montcalm wrote his famous letter of surrender to James Wolfe, not knowing that Wolfe himself had died, as Montcalm himself would here at five in the morning. **45, rue Saint-Louis; now shops and apartments.**

**L'Asile Finlay** 1860-1970. Designed by Stent & Laver.

The Anglican Church built this as an asylum for the elderly and also a home for orphans, right on the edge of town. Its Ottawa architects—who also originally designed the East and West Blocks of Parliament Hill—created a strangely playful Gothic Revival structure with several colours of stone, a steeply pitched attic, and the requisite pointed arches, high-spirited Victorian architecture that seemed to invite hauntings. **200, chemin Sainte-Foy; now a government office tower.**

---

**Cinéma Français** 1911-1948

This corner had long been a place of entertainment: a pub and inn stood here from 1678 until 1840. By the 1920s it was a cinema with a live orchestra playing under the management of Roméo Labbé de Limoilou, though the owner was his wife, Julia Bilodeau de Saint-Sauveur. The theatre survived three fires in its first decades, and then was replaced by a deco movie house, the Laurier. **296, rue Saint-Vallier.**

### Cinéma Laurier 1950-1974
Designed by Etienne Begin.

Replacing the Cinéma Français, the new, $250,000 cinema advertised its "scientifically controlled acoustics," "cycloramic screen," and smoking room. All this modernity expressed itself on the exterior in the form of skyscraping vertical fins and a protruding neon sign. The Laurier was torn down for a city parking lot. **296, rue Saint-Vallier.**

---

### L'Église St-Vincent-de-Paul 1898-2010
Designed by Francois Xavier Berlinguet.

The Society of St-Vincent-de-Paul, a missionary organization that aims to help the poor, set up shop here in 1861. Berlinguet, a woodcarver's son who became a distinguished architect and civil engineer, designed this church in 1898. A fire left only its facade, but it was soon rebuilt and could hold five hundred people. Much of the society's complex was knocked down in 1971 for the new autoroute Dufferin-Montmorency. Only the church facade remained, alone, until it too was demolished.
**804, côte d'Abraham.**

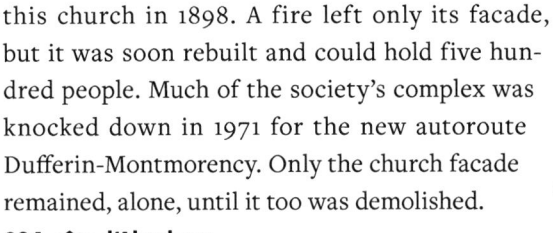

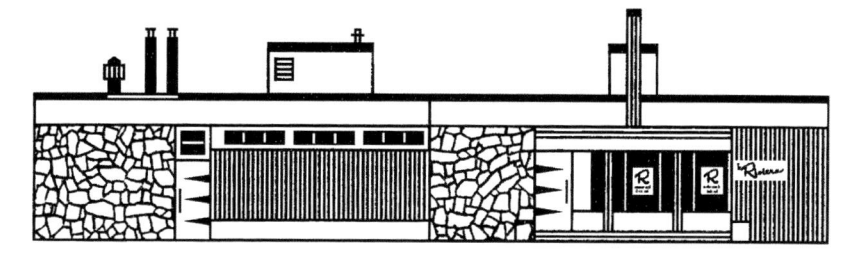

## Riviera Restaurant 1950s-1967

Quebec City's first restaurant to open 24/7, an art deco white stucco shed that got a modernist makeover of stone and wood around 1960. It was built over the river and was technically outside city limits (and the reach of city tax assessors). Known for its spaghetti, the restaurant was lost to a late-night fire in 1967. **30, rue Dalhousie.**

---

## L'Hôtel Louis-XIV 1903-1966

Place Royale was a landmark in the history of French settlement in Quebec City, dating from the mid-1600s. After a fire in 1682, the area was rebuilt using perhaps the earliest fire code in North America, which dictated stone walls along the property lines. Ironically, this later building was destroyed by fire, an event that helped spur the preservation and restoration of the area.

**Place Royale.**

## L'Église Saint-Joseph 1941-2012

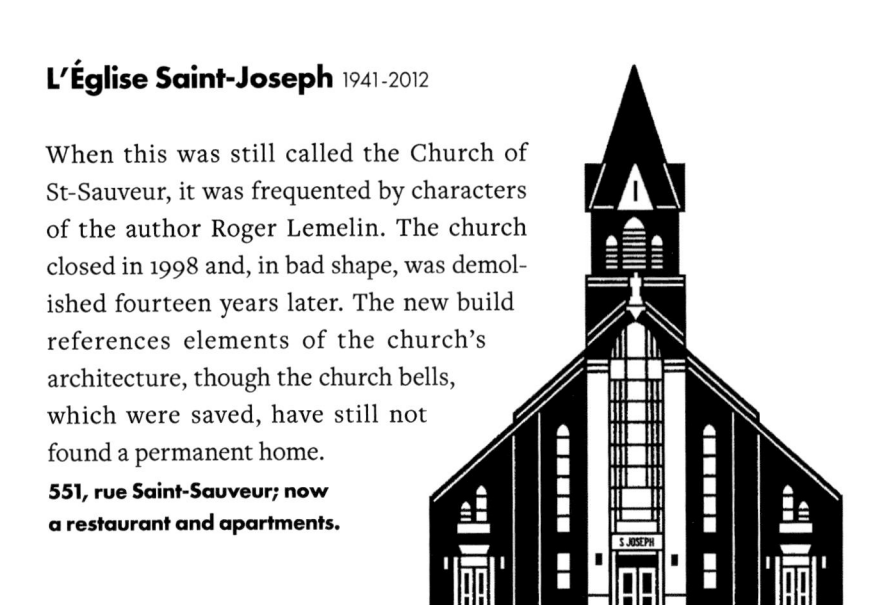

When this was still called the Church of St-Sauveur, it was frequented by characters of the author Roger Lemelin. The church closed in 1998 and, in bad shape, was demolished fourteen years later. The new build references elements of the church's architecture, though the church bells, which were saved, have still not found a permanent home.

**551, rue Saint-Sauveur; now a restaurant and apartments.**

## Le Domaine Spencer Wood 1863-1966

This estate created in the late eighteenth century was called Powell Place by its British owner in 1780, then Spencer Wood in 1815. Reconstructed in 1860 as a neoclassical mansion, it became the official residence of Quebec's lieutenant-governors, gaining a front portico along the way for added grandeur. In 1950, it was renamed Bois de Coulonge in an assertion of Quebec's francophone identity. The mansion burned in 1966; Lieutenant-Governor Paul Comtois died in the fire while trying to rescue a religious artifact.

**Now parc du Bois-de-Coulonge.**

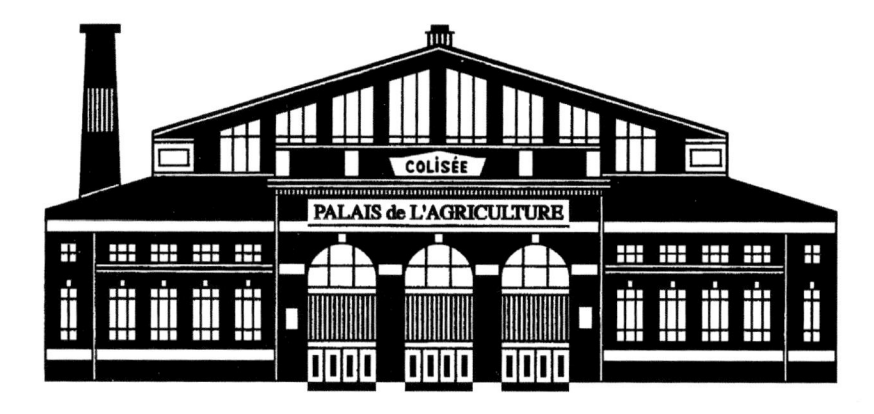

**Palais de l'Agriculture** 1930-1949. Designed by Raoul Chenevert.

Originally built on the city's exhibition grounds for agricultural displays, this building was fitted out in 1942 as an arena, home to two junior hockey teams. It hosted many major events in its short life, including celebrations for the end of the Second World War. A 1949 fire, which started in the "millionaires' section," reduced the building to ashes. Pieces of its facade were reused in its replacement, now known as the Pavillon de la Jeunesse.
**250, boulevard Wilfrid-Hamel.**

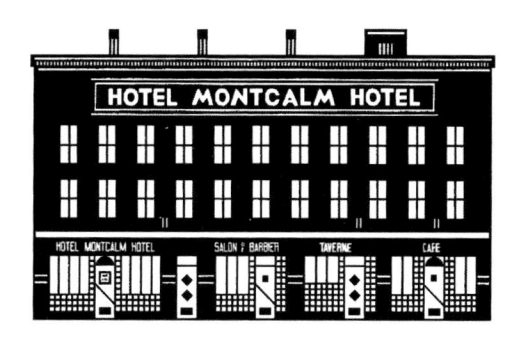

## Hotel Montcalm

1912-1969. Probably designed by J.S. Bergeron.

Albert-Joseph Pelland purchased a hardware store on place d'Youville around 1910 and replaced it with a hotel that would define the square for half a century. Its frontage included the hotel, a barbershop, a tavern, and a café, each of which by the 1940s had a sleek painted sign surrounded by glass block. Pelland lasted forty years at the helm, and the hotel itself was brought down only by the municipal reconstruction of the square.
**Rue Saint-Jean and rue des Glacis; now place d'Youville bus terminal.**

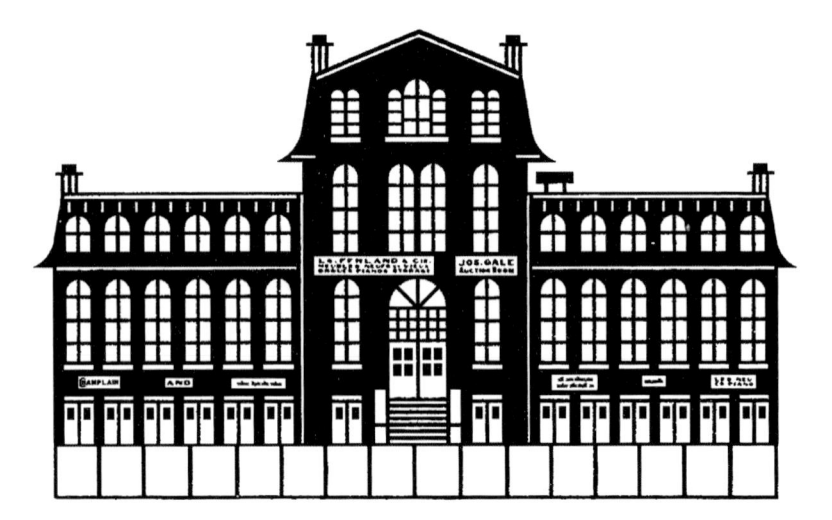

## Halle Montcalm 1877-1931
Designed by Paul Cousin; redesigned by Robitaille & Desmeules.

In 1877, architect Paul Cousin designed a new city market to be built from the stones of the city's old fortifications. Downstairs were mostly meat vendors, and upstairs was a meeting hall. The mansard-roofed structure operated for half a century, but in 1929 public markets were losing their importance; the old building was plastered with signs and billboards. The city chose to rebuild it as Palais Montcalm, which then included a library and swimming pool. **995, rue d'Youville; now Palais Montcalm.**

---

## L'Hôtel Saint-Roch 1914-1974
Designed by Ludger Robitaille.

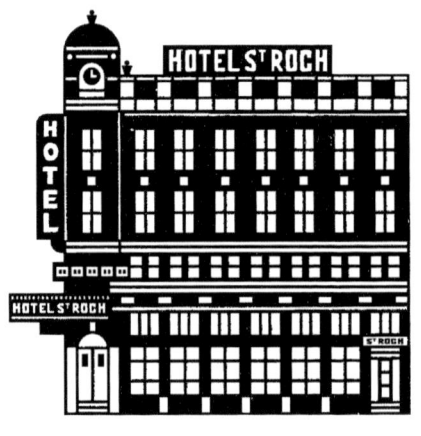

When it opened, this was the best hotel in the lower town, its stone colonnade facing a square with a statue of Cartier. It burned in 1923 but was rebuilt a year later, advertisements trumpeting its new, fireproof construction. By 1950 a room cost three dollars, and the hotel was well on its way to its final down-at-heel years. It was demolished as part of a "revitalization," and in 1983 its place was filled by a library, which itself is being revitalized.
**350, rue Saint-Joseph Est; now Bibliothèque Gabrielle-Roy.**

**Hippodrome de Québec** 1917-2012. Designed by Tanguay & Lebon.

This site housed a racetrack as early as 1898, and in the 1910s it became home to Quebec's Agricultural Exhibition. (Along the way, the first airplane landing in the city happened here.) The building's architecture looked back to the Romanesque of the Chicago 1893 Columbian Exposition. Horse races, baseball, and even the Formula Atlantic Grand Prix de Québec passed through here. The site is now home to a different sort of entertainment.
**Boulevard Wilfrid-Hamel; now Centre Vidéotron.**

---

## L'Ancien Hôtel de Ville
1795-1896

Thomas Aston Coffin was British civil secretary and controller of public accounts for lower Canada and, like many colonial officials, a busy land speculator. He built this mansion in the Palladian style for himself. A generation later, in 1842, this rather British neoclassical structure became the home of city government. In 1896 city hall moved a few blocks to a purpose-built home, where it remains. The old building was replaced by row houses. **78, rue Saint-Louis.**

## Girls' High School

1878-1970. Expanded 1914 by Harry and Edward Black Staveley.

This Second Empire greystone pile began as a small high school for Protestant girls. It was expanded in 1914, despite the waning of the area's anglophone population, and combined into Quebec High School, which moved offsite in the 1940s. The government purchased the old school, and it became part of the parliamentary complex. It was demolished in 1970 to build a tunnel between the parliament and other government buildings. **Now parc de la Francophonie.**

---

## L'Entrepôt de la Compagnie Paquet 1890s-1970s

The company was named for Zéphirin Paquet, a former milkman, but it was his wife Marie-Louise Hamel who built the business, starting with a shop for hats and other clothing. It became a wildly successful department store, bringing mail-order catalogues, order by phone, delivery services, and even Santa Claus to Quebec. This large warehouse suggested the scale of the Paquet operation, while its sign advertised to passersby on the adjacent bridge. **95, rue de la Pointe-aux-Lièvres; now an apartment building.**

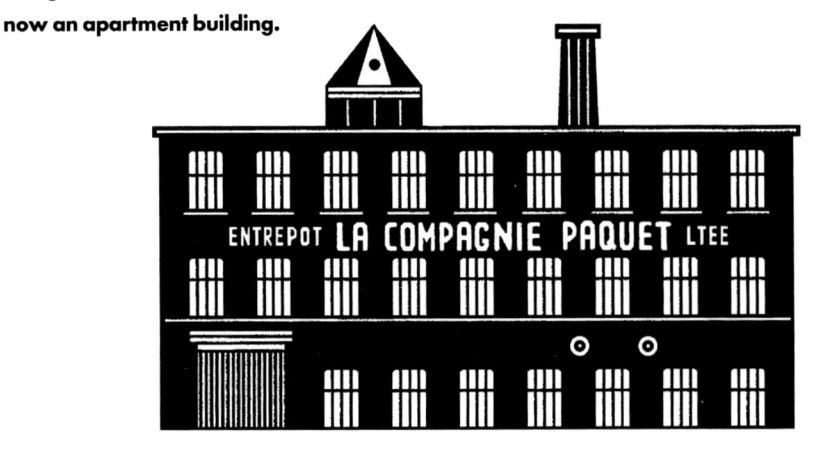

## Le Pavillon d'Aiguillon de l'Hôtel-Dieu 1889-1954
Designed by Georges-Émile Tanguay.

The Hôtel-Dieu was the first permanent hospital in either Canada or the United States, founded in 1637. Tanguay's building was a major expansion and modernization of the hospital. The architect emphasized natural light and ventilation, though the conservative facades mixed Romanesque with a steep chateau-style roof. At its opening, a journalist called it "a palace for the ill." The operating room was surrounded by glass and fully lit by natural light, but stained glass replaced the clear glass after a few years, as the sun was getting in the surgeons' eyes. The building was replaced by a fourteen-storey tower, which helped spur heritage regulation for the hospital in 1963. **75-77, rue des Remparts.**

# SHERBROOKE, Quebec

The town of Sherbrooke began as a trading post for furs, where the Saint-François and Magog Rivers come together. Its buildings have combined French and Anglo-American traditions, but, as across the Eastern Townships, the English voice speaks louder in the architecture. The city has evolved from a manufacturing town to one of universities and government, and downtown has seen its fortunes fall and rise. Some landmarks have been lost along the way.

## Hôtel Wellington 1928-2017

Built during the heyday of downtown with some ostentatious classical detailing, this hotel expanded decades later. It was still going strong into the middle of the century, with a barber, an indoor pool, and live music at the neon-decorated bar, the Flamingo. Louis Armstrong stopped in, and local musicians knew that if you played "la Well," you were for real. The hotel survived two fires, but eventually went downmarket and closed.

**68, rue Wellington Sud; now Espace Centro.**

## Cinéma de Paris
1948-1988. Designed by Jean-Julien Perrault.

The Premier Theatre opened on this site in 1917, and in 1933 it reopened as the Cinéma de Paris. A 1948 rebuild delivered a very modern Vitrolite tile facade and a round sign reaching out over the street, its handwritten lettering borrowing from French graphic arts of the time. It was demolished in 1984 but has been memorialized in a trompe-l'oeil mural.
**372, rue King Ouest; now a parking lot.**

---

## Château Frontenac 1906-1964

The businessman Achille Joncas built this grand country hotel in the Queen Anne style, which was fashionable here and elsewhere. A large tower and cupola marked the corner and porticoes stretched along its two facades, once painted green. By the 1950s its clientele were less privileged, and in 1959 its manager was charged with running a bawdy house. It closed and burned in 1964.
**Rue Wellington Sud and rue Aberdeen.**

## GUELPH, Ontario

From the time it was first colonized, Guelph was built with a vision. The Crown chartered the Canada Company to settle a huge area of Ontario. Company superintendent John Galt set up shop here and drew an unusual plan for the town: it began with a wedge shape at a bend in the Speed River, its streets spilling outward before assuming a more regular pattern. After the Grand Trunk Railroad arrived in the 1850s, the village began to grow in sophistication, often building with the local limestone. New arrivals, including talented architects, rose to the challenge of the Old World-ish town plan and Guelph's relatively outsize cultural and financial strength.

### Canadian Bank of Commerce 1884-1968
Designed by David B. Dick.

Dick was a prominent Scottish-Torontonian architect who shaped much of the early University of Toronto. When the Bank of Commerce brought him to Guelph, he designed a corner branch in the Scottish Baronial style, with a mansard roof and a small cone-roofed tower. After the merger that created CIBC, it was demolished in 1968 — along with most of the block — and replaced by a modern bank building that still stands. **59 Wyndham Street North.**

**Guelph Public Library** 1905-1964. Designed by William Frye Colwill.

Like many ambitious towns in the first decade of the twentieth century, Guelph set out to build a library and asked the Carnegie Foundation for support. The Americans were interested, but they saw a problem: its Beaux-Arts design was too "grandiloquent and expensive" for the place. Colwill, a Welshman who had settled in town a few years earlier, designed a structure that followed the busy neoclassicism of the Beaux-Arts school, with ornate capitals and corbels, but which had its main door at the corner—an unusually asymmetrical choice. It would be faced with artificial "Roman stone," a state-of-the-art product made of precast concrete. Guelph's library board went ahead, and this grandiloquent building was wrecked in 1964 and replaced by the current library building. **100 Norfolk Street; now Guelph Public Library.**

**Royal Opera House** 1873-1953. Designed by Harry J. Powell.

An opera house was another Victorian badge of sophistication. Citizens of Guelph invested in a civic company to build this one, and in grand style: the hall had 1,200 seats when Guelph had only eleven thousand residents. They hired Stratford architect Harry Powell to design it, and the Ancient Order of United Workmen constructed it with five storefronts and an upstairs meeting hall. Opera didn't pay the bills, and by the 1920s this was a beloved movie house, the Capitol. But in the 1950s Guelph purged nearly all the Victorian buildings on St. George Square (including the Bank of Commerce). The opera house was torn down to build the Simpsons-Sears department store, since repurposed for medical use. **Wyndham Street at Woolwich Street; now Guelph Community Health Centre.**

# HAMILTON, Ontario

Once known as the Birmingham of Canada and now as Steeltown, Hamilton has long been a place where people make things. It also has a remarkable natural geography, with a harbour ideal (after the construction of a canal) for commerce and defence, and an escarpment that pressed its people and enterprises tightly together. Its built form is rich and varied. Yet the twentieth century saw much of it damaged by forces from without and within. Deindustrialization stripped the city's architecture as well as its livelihoods. Local politicians followed the path of urban renewal to level forty acres of downtown. And, of course, the universal forces of changing architectural taste, changes in popular entertainment, and the inescapable element of fire altered the city's fabric. Hamilton has a wealth of buildings, but it has lost much.

## Spectator Building
1898-1950s
Designed by William P. Witton.

"The Spec" was founded in 1846, and having outlasted its rivals, it is a powerful institution in the city. For decades it was based in the heart of downtown on James, in a six-storey Edwardian classical loft that included a gym for newspaper staff. The Spectator moved to King Street in 1920, and its former home was eventually replaced by a Royal Bank building, itself demolished in 2001. **28-32 James Street.**

## Malcolm & Souter Furniture Company 1872-1969
Building extension by Stewart & Witton, 1910.

In the mid-nineteenth century, the sewing machine transformed domestic life in North America and set off a huge boom in manufacturing, with accompanying American legal fights over patents that were known as the Sewing Machine War. Meanwhile, manufacturers in Canada were free to ignore American patents, and Richard Wanzer set up a large factory on this spot to spin out his popular Little Wanzer model, while he and his partner fought workers' attempts to achieve a nine-hour day. The company went bust in 1890, and furniture makers Malcolm & Souter took over the building for three generations of production. **Northeast corner of Barton and Mary Streets; now a parking lot.**

---

## Kresge Building 1930-2017. Addition and alterations, 1948.
Designed by Garnet McElroy.

The discount retailer Kresge's, in Hamilton and elsewhere, built in style. For this shop opposite Gore Park, the company's Canadian architect, McElroy of Windsor, dressed up a two-storey building with two-dimensional stone ziggurats set into its yellow brick. Kresge's evolved into Kmart, and this became a bingo hall. Now, with the growth of downtown, it's the site of two high-rise towers with bargain-basement architecture on their street facade.

**43-51 King Street East; now Cobalt Residences.**

Ontario

## Hamilton Public Library

1889-1955. Designed by William Stewart.

Perhaps the first purpose-built library in the province, this was a highly ornate late-Victorian house of knowledge. Prominent local architect Stewart decorated it with applied stone arches, elaborate corbelling, a corner tower, and a forest of turrets. The library moved one block into a new Carnegie-funded building in 1913. (This is now the city's family courthouse; HAMILTON PUBLIC LIBRARY remains carved into its facade.) The next year, the older structure became the first home to the Hamilton Municipal Gallery, which would become the Art Gallery of Hamilton. **22 Main Street West; now a commercial building.**

## Mercury Mills

1917-1983. Designed by Charles T. Main.

At the height of the textile industry in Hamilton, John Penman came to town from Paris, Ontario, and established an operation that would employ well over a thousand people. Its main plant, located here on a rail line, featured all the architectural language of Detroit Fordism, with reinforced-concrete structure and walls of windows. Hundreds of workers — many of them women — produced hosiery, underwear, and other products until the plant closed in 1955; the behemoth was demolished a quarter-century later. **South side of Cumberland Avenue between Gage and Prospect Avenues; now housing.**

**T.H. & B. Station** 1895-1933. Designed by W. & W. Stewart.

The Toronto, Hamilton & Buffalo was a local railway that (while mostly owned by the Canadian Pacific Railway and New York Central) operated separate freight and passenger service for about a century. For its first main station, the father-and-son local architects employed the popular Richardsonian Romanesque style, with cut stone at the base, red brick above, and a tall corner turret. The station was replaced in 1933 by its Stream-line Moderne successor, which remains.

**Hunter Street near Hughson Street South; now Hamilton Centre GO Station.**

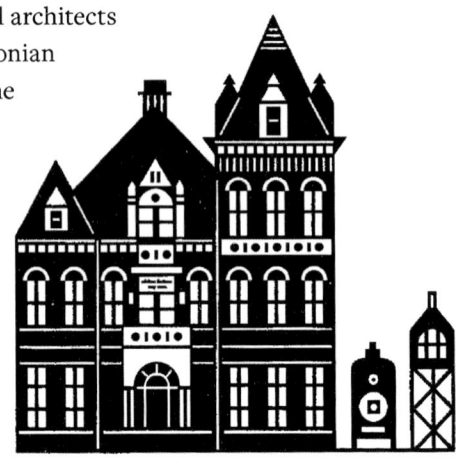

---

**Century Theatre** 1913-2010. Designed by Lempert & Son.

When the Lyric Theatre opened in 1913, it was the fifth large theatre in Hamilton presenting vaudeville acts. The new theatre's promised amenities included a men's smoking room, a ladies' waiting room, and "a nursery for babies in arms." A Romanesque facade fronted a massive structure that extended 190 feet back, containing seats for two thousand people, indirect lighting, and air conditioning. The theatre soon shifted to movies—five theatres were too many—and was renamed the Century. It was renovated several times and kept showing films until it closed in 1989, starting a long period of vacancy and decline.

**12 Mary Street.**

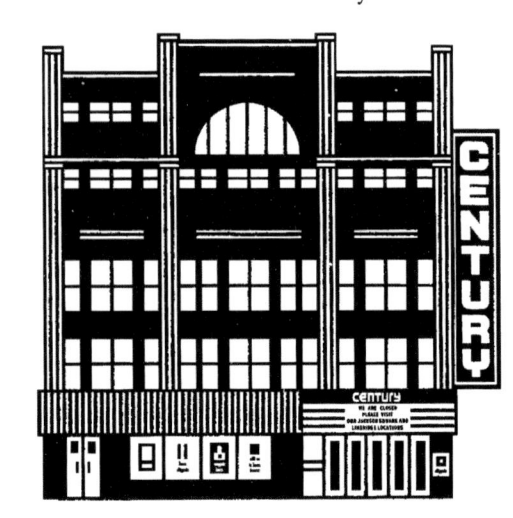

## Birks Building 1883-1972

Designed by Richard Waite.

Insurance companies (like banks) often used architecture to send a message of solidity and durability. This office for the Canada Life Assurance Company certainly seemed like the kind of place you could trust with your family's future: its massive masonry walls weren't going anywhere, and the hierarchy of its arched windows suggested order and sophistication. And yet the tower at the corner was turned at an angle, in a playful twist by the architect, Buffalonian Richard Waite. (Waite also designed the provincial legislative buildings at Queen's Park in Toronto.) Canada Life moved to Toronto in the twenties, and this became the Birks Building; the jewellers installed a mechanical "clock of the changing horsemen," which helped make the building a landmark. The clock was saved when the building was wrecked, to much protest, in 1972. **King and James Streets; now Commerce Place.**

---

## Majestic Restaurant 1933-1969

The era of urban renewal hit Hamilton hard. Councillors saw the old downtown as declining, and an outside planner (Murray Jones, the former head of the Metro Toronto Planning Board) suggested the *au courant* solution of wiping out the entire Market Square area for what became Jackson Square. Two hundred and sixty businesses were closed and demolished, including this diner run by Macedonian immigrant Dan Kuzoff. The Majestic had a flashy facade of neon, Vitrolite tile, and octagonal windows. The mall does not.

**7-8 Market Square; now Jackson Square.**

## Royal Hamilton Yacht Club 1891-1915. Designed by William Stewart.

"Hamilton's sporting organizations have always done well," reported Toronto's *Globe* in 1891, and it is "a port from which hails a very large proportion of the greyhounds of the lakes." That year, the thriving local yacht club's fleet included *Psyche* and *Samoa*; the club was led by senator (and alleged price-fixer of military uniforms) W.E. Sanford. Its new clubhouse featured a bowling alley and a twelve-foot-deep veranda on three sides, its ornate fretwork apparently painted in lively colours. The clubhouse would burn two decades later.
**Burlington Beach, facing Hamilton Harbour.**

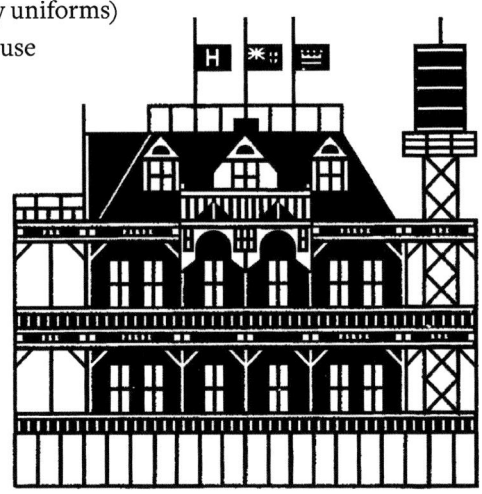

## Palace Theatre 1920-1972. Designed by Thomas Lamb.

When it opened as the Pantages, with 2,007 seats, this was among the biggest theatres in the country. Lamb, its architect, was a New York theatre specialist who would design Radio City Music Hall. Lamb's design was very urbane: a narrow entrance fronted on King, flanked by shops, and you walked through a colonnaded corridor to reach the theatre itself at the back of the block. The theatre was a wonderland of playful classicism, with medallions and rosettes on every wall, columns and niches at every turn—an interior that was ready for magic, of stage and screen.
**137 King Street East.**

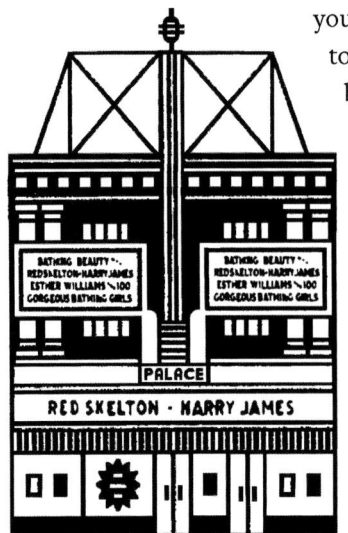

**Ontario**

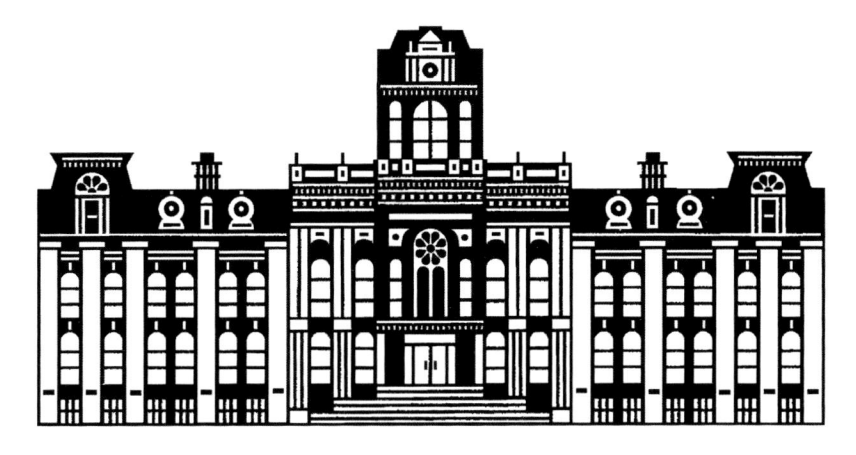

**Wentworth County Courthouse** 1878-1956. Designed by Charles Mulligan.

When George Hamilton laid out his plan for the town, Prince's Square was part of his vision. When a district courthouse was awarded to Hamilton—a huge boon to Mr. Hamilton's real estate interests—he donated the land for that square and the adjacent courthouse. Half a century later the courthouse was replaced by this grander structure, designed by Mulligan in the symmetrical, mansard-roofed, and textured idiom of Second Empire. Mulligan, a Brit, spent fifteen years in Hamilton and built widely in the area before leaving for Chicago. (One of his full buildings, at 185 Young Street, survives intact.) The courthouse made it to the 1950s, but not beyond. A consultant wrote, "It is not a modern building, but it has spirit and tradition." It was replaced by a modern courthouse. Some of its columns still stand in White Chapel Memorial Gardens. **50 Main Street East; now the Provincial Offences Administration Building.**

## Hamilton Normal School
1906-1953
Designed by Francis R. Heakes.

A normal school was what we now call a teachers' college, and Ontario built four of them in the years around 1907, all to very similar designs, as the province moved to upgrade and standardize teacher training. Hamilton's faced Victoria Park, and like its siblings it was a brick box with a portico out front, an entrance at the corner, and a copper-clad dome up top. It burned down on New Year's Day, 1953; one of its siblings survives in Stratford. **Strathcona Avenue and Lamoureaux Street; now apartments.**

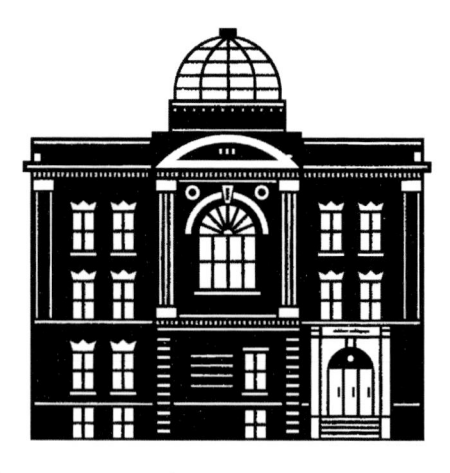

---

## Grand Opera House 1880-1961. Designed by George H. Lalor.

Designed by a young Toronto architect, this hall began with theatre and made it through vaudeville to the movie era. The massive brick volume of the hall was wrapped by a smaller Second Empire-style building that contained a hotel. Like other similar venues, it quickly lost its original purpose in the 1920s (having meanwhile hosted some boxing matches) and was converted to a movie house. It took on a series of names: the Grand, the Granada, the Downtown. It closed in 1961 and was demolished as downtown streets were reengineered for the car.
**James and Wilson Streets; now a shopping plaza.**

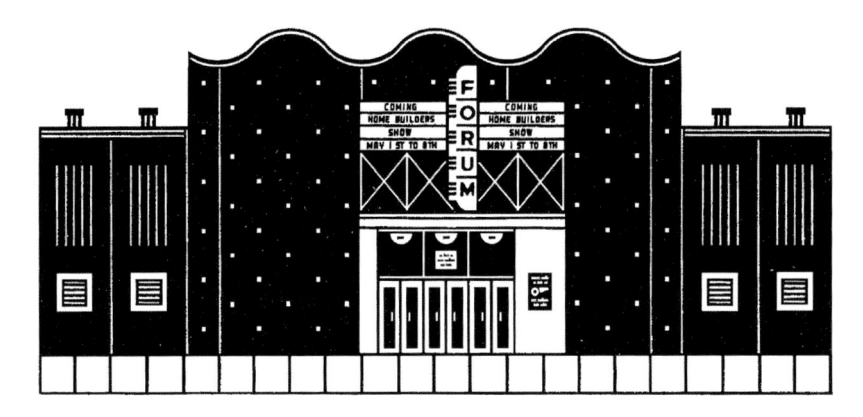

## Hamilton Forum 1913-1977

First known as the Barton Street Arena, this was a rink typical of its generation, with awkward sightlines, small dressing rooms, and unreliable ice. It housed the NHL's Hamilton Tigers in the 1920s but was better known (after a midcentury renovation and name change) as a junior hockey barn with raucous crowds and teams ready to scrap. The junior team's owners renamed the squad the Fincups, an awkward play on their own last names, and the slogan "Follow the Fincups" was painted out front. In 1976 the ice-making machinery broke down, and the Fincups followed a trail out of town. The arena was torn down the same year. **500 Barton Street East; now houses.**

## Barton Street Jail 1875-1978

From the street, it looked nearly domestic, if you didn't notice the bars on the windows. Two gabled, stone-fronted wings addressed the street, flanking a portico and long stair. The square watchtower hiding behind the gables, however, told a truer story. This was a place of imprisonment and death: eight people were executed here between 1876 and 1953. The old jail was demolished after the current detention centre was finished next door; some of its stones survive at the parking lot of the Battle of Stoney Creek National Historic Site. **165 Barton Street East; now Hamilton-Wentworth Detention Centre.**

**Ontario**

**City Hall** 1890-1961. Designed by James Balfour.

Hamilton's second city hall followed the fashion of the moment, borrowing the Romanesque language of American architect H.H. Richardson. (It was very similar to the Toronto city hall being designed at the same time.) Its rounded arches, rusticated sandstone, and corner clock tower created an air of classical virtue and rustic grandeur. In the postwar period, there were predictable calls for a more modern city hall, and Eaton's wanted the land. So, in 1961, Hamilton completed the modernist city hall by Stanley Roscoe that survives today and a remarkable school-board building that was demolished in 2012. After the old city hall was torn down, some of its stone became fill for the wharf at the foot of Catharine Street, where the HMCS *Haida* is docked. The bell from the city hall tower rests in the Hamilton City Centre shopping mall. **James Street; now Hamilton City Centre.**

**Bank of Hamilton** 1892-1985
Designed by Richard Waite; expanded by Charles Mills.

Not just a bank but a headquarters in a skyscraper. Originally three storeys by the Buffalo architect Waite, this structure was remade in 1907 as a tower of eight floors with a proper base, middle, and top—as the leading skyscraper designer of the day, Louis Sullivan, would have suggested. Mills, a local architect, went on to design ten branches for the Bank of Hamilton in four provinces. The bank ran into trouble in the 1920s and merged into the Bank of Commerce, and the tower eventually belonged to CIBC, which modernized and then demolished it. **King and James Streets; now Commerce Place.**

# KINGSTON, Ontario

The presence of government and the military shaped this city almost from the start. It was, though briefly, capital of the United Province of Canada in the 1840s. Accordingly most of its early architecture spoke in colonial idioms, first neoclassical and then Victorian Gothic and eclectic. (Traces of French fortifications remain at Fort Frontenac.) The main medium was initially local limestone, followed by brick. In the twentieth century, the growth of Queen's University gave Kingston new vitality and brought a variety of architectural ideas to campus and to town. That meant new architectural expressions, some of which, though young, have already been erased.

---

**Sugarman Building** 1964-1999. Designed by Drever & Smith.

Here was a little slab of modernism facing Market Square. Starting in the 1950s, the architect Mies van der Rohe channelled his brand of modernist into corporate offices such as the TD Centre in Toronto. Here, architect Ernest Cromarty (of the local firm Drever & Smith) borrowed from Mies to design a tiny, rigorous office building for the Sugarman family. Radical for Kingston in 1964, it was demolished before its fortieth birthday and, posthumously, received a civic design award.

**16 Brock Street;
now a parking lot.**

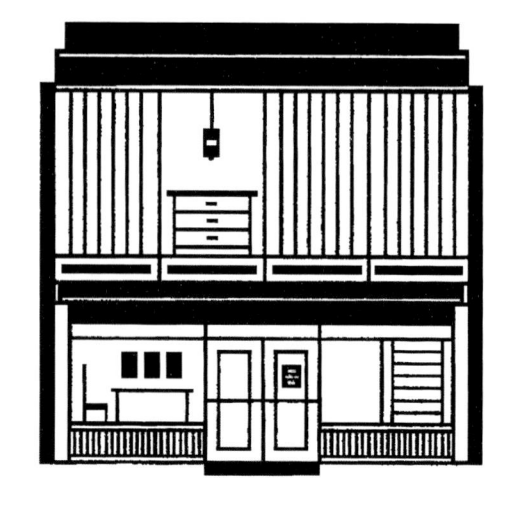

**British American Hotel** 1791-1963

One of the city's longest-lived buildings was constructed as the Kingston Hotel in 1791, in fine Georgian style. A century later it was still good enough for visiting dignitaries Charles Dickens and Oscar Wilde. (However, a local newspaper reported that when Wilde arrived, one afternoon in 1882, "he advanced in a listless and languid manner to the hotel stairs. He climbed these as if enduring a most terrible punishment." His lecture on beauty received a mixed reaction.) The hotel burned down in 1963.
**King and Clarence Streets.**

## Beth Israel Synagogue
1910-1961. Designed by Power & Son.

Kingston has had a Jewish community since the mid-1800s, and around 1900 three small groups came together to build this, the city's first synagogue. Donations from local churches helped pay for a local architect's design. Like many synagogues of its time, this combined classical symmetry borrowed from German architecture with quotations from Moorish architecture (in this case, the shape of its domes). In the 1960s the older merchant congregation grew with the arrival of Jewish professors at Queen's, and a modernist new synagogue was built on Centre Street. The old site is now a parking lot named after a synagogue member, businessman Sam Springer. **148 Queen Street.**

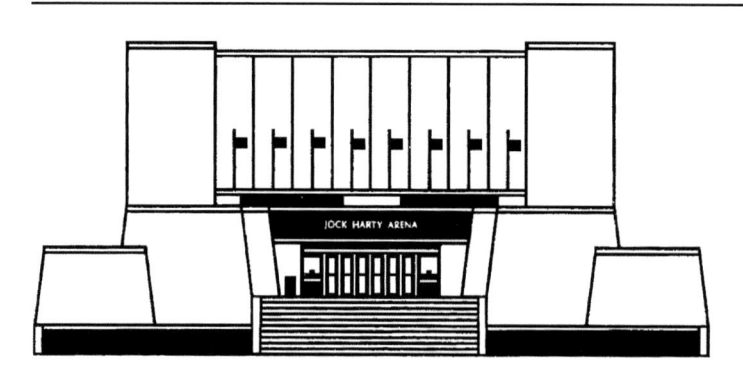

## Jock Harty Arena 1970-2007

John "Jock" Harty was a Queen's hockey star of the 1890s (on a team that once beat Yale, a big accomplishment). He became a prominent local doctor and businessman, and his name was attached to three generations of ice rinks at the university. This, the third, mixed rough-cut limestone with great slabs of precast concrete. It was designed on a modernist idea of combining uses: it held a rink, an indoor running track, and six rooftop tennis courts. For decades this is where Queen's students wrote final exams and then celebrated their convocations. It was itself replaced by the nearby Queen's Centre, which includes a large sports facility. **69 Union Street West; now Mitchell Hall at Queen's.**

# KITCHENER, Ontario

Before it was Kitchener, this was Berlin. German-speaking settlers, at first Pennsylvania Dutch, set the tone of the place, including its irregular street pattern and fieldstone buildings. After it incorporated as a city (and changed its name), it grew rapidly and blended German and Swiss influences, factories and houses cheek-by-jowl. The twentieth century brought TVs and modern architecture. As the city and the region shifted from smokestacks to suburban and high-tech, some things have been lost along the way.

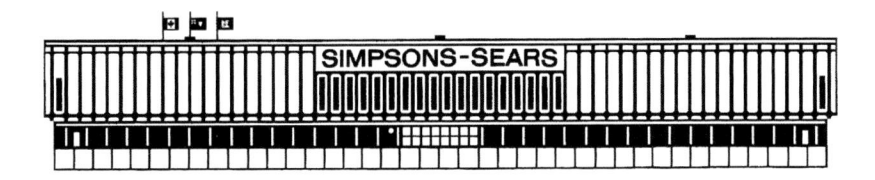

**Sears** 1965-2019. Designed by Maxwell Miller.

The shopping mall is a product of the modern era, and the first generation of malls often featured boldly modernist architecture. This Canadian Sears (designed by the company's in-house architect) was a sculptural store, capping an expanse of green glazed brick with modules of precast concrete that formed a steady drumbeat of oval-inside-rectangle. In this way its facades chased the same goals of seriality and abstraction as contemporary artists of the time—but at Sears. After the store went bankrupt in early 2018, the mall's owners replaced the store with a new wing whose architecture imitates a Victorian brick-and-beam factory. A few precast panels remain as relics of a vanished era. **2960 Kingsway Drive; now CF Fairview Park.**

## Barra Castle 1930-2010

A tall and stentorian Tudor structure that eventually picked up the vibe of a late-movie haunted house. Its name, printed above the door, was taken from a Scottish castle, which the Kitchener building did not much resemble. It was an apartment building for most if not all of its life, before tenants were cleared out in 2007 for their own safety. Local urban legends about its former owner, Molly Marquette, accumulated; for instance, that she had commissioned the building to look like a Russian castle where she had grown up. **393 Queen Street South; now a condo building.**

---

## Electrohome Plant 4 1898-2020

This was a loft building that saw a lot of change. It was constructed in 1898 by Leander Klippert for his Diamond Furniture Company, Mr. Klippert having learned the business from his father, who built furniture and coffins. The building passed into other hands, including Murawsky Furniture, before Electrohome bought it in the early 1950s. This was a local business known Canada-wide for making TVs, both the attractive wooden cabinets and the electronic guts. (Though no coffins.) Electrohome called the building Plant 4 and made furniture and appliances there before selling the building in 1968. Their painted sign remained on the brick for another forty years, long after the company itself had vanished. **152 Shanley Street; now a development site.**

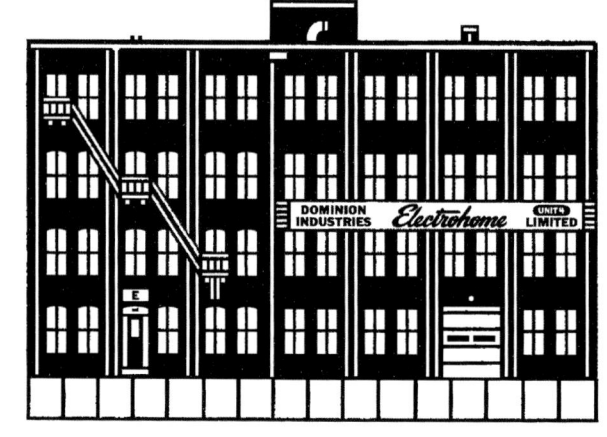

## LONDON, Ontario

In 1793, John Graves Simcoe named London and the Thames River; he suggested the city as Upper Canada's capital. York (later Toronto) won that title, but London became the seat of its district. In 1827 the construction of what's now the Middlesex County Courthouse provided stone evidence of the city's emergence. The city grew, spurred by the military, fertile farmland, and the presence of the railway. Builders used Ontario styles and local London stock brick, often described as "white brick"—an architectural echo of that other London.

---

### Hotel London 1927-1972

This eight-storey Romanesque Revival pile opened on a corner site in the heart of downtown in the midst of the 1920s boom. Advertisements claimed its accommodations were "modern in every way." For more than four decades the hotel hosted conventions, meetings, and major social events, including a New Year's gala. It closed after St. Patrick's Day in 1972, brought down for a new $25-million hotel-office redevelopment—big news at a time when the suburbs were starting to boom and the city thought it needed something more modern.

**Dundas and Wellington Streets; now City Centre.**

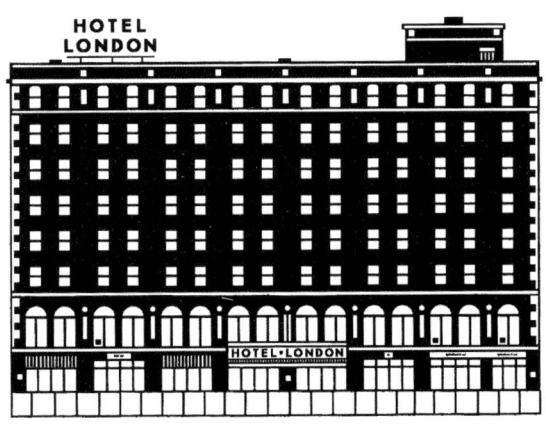

**YMCA Building** 1897-1981. Designed by Moore & Henry.

London had one of Canada's first branches of the Young Men's Christian Association, only a dozen years after that group was founded in Britain to mix religious evangelism with sports. (James Naismith invented basketball at a YMCA in 1891.) This London centre was officially opened to the public on New Year's Day, 1897. Its architecture mixed a Romanesque Revival entrance with pointy Gothic towers. Arson in early 1981 gutted the building, and it was soon demolished. **Wellington Street and Queens Avenue; now One London Place.**

---

**Victory Building** 1930-1978

Originally home to Bell Telephone, this deco tower marked London's centre of commerce, standing next to the similarly ambitious Hotel London. Its rectangular windows dissolved at the top into arched windows and then zigzags that pointed skyward. The building later housed a RCAF recruiting centre and acquired the name Victory Building. Less dramatically, the Northern Life Assurance Company took it over as their headquarters and tore it down in 1978.
**Wellington Street; now a parking lot at City Centre.**

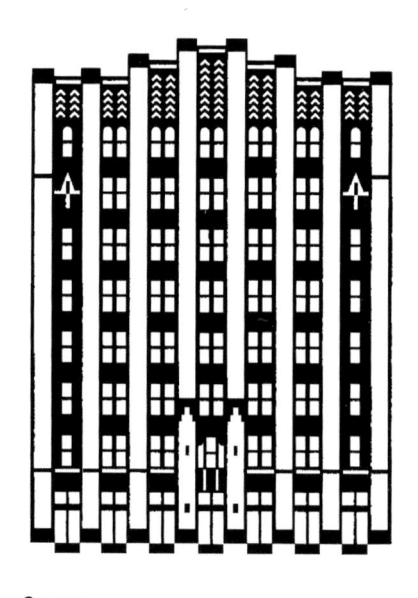

**Ontario** 88

## OSHAWA, Ontario

Oshawa was incorporated as a village in 1849, its name taken from an Anishinaabemowin word for the point at which one transfers from a canoe to walking. The emphasis on transportation was prescient. The harbour, Port Sydenham, linked Oshawa to the world—until the railway came in 1856. This opened the door to industry like Robert McLaughlin's McLaughlin Carriage Company, and when the McLaughlin family got into the automotive business, in what became General Motors Canada, they set the town's course for the century to come. Huge industrial complexes reshaped much of the city. The car also influenced Oshawa's urban form, as it did almost everywhere else; the city spread out to the north and west. And sometimes, still, an old building is wrecked to make way for a new parking lot.

---

### Conant House 1873-1985

Named Buena Vista, this Italianate house served as the homestead to the Conant family—the second home, after this Loyalist-descended family first settled near the port around 1800. Thomas Conant wrote two books, *Upper Canada Sketches* and *Life in Canada*, that tell all about this history. His son Gordon made history as mayor of Oshawa and, very briefly, the twelfth premier of Ontario. **Now Conant Place, 1050 Simcoe Street South.**

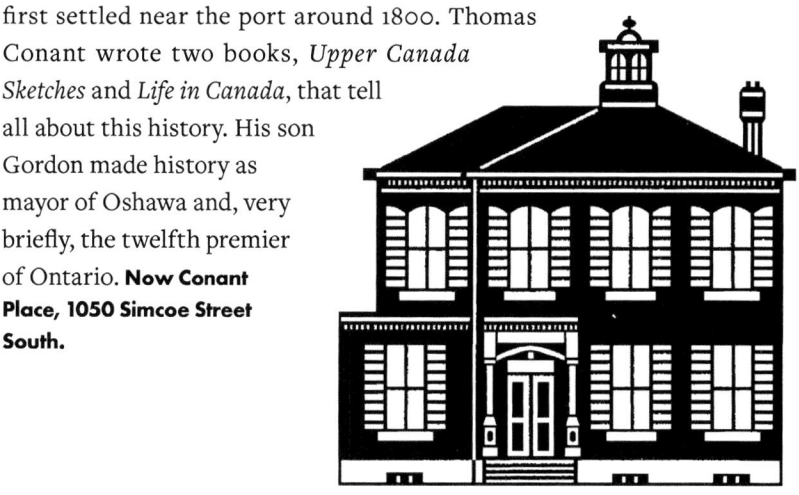

## Mayfair Bowling Alley 1930s-1957

In the 1920s and '30s, bowling was among the most popular sports in the country. (A Canadian, Thomas Ryan, had invented the five-pin version in his Toronto bowling alley.) Oshawa's Mayfair was a sharp deco building with porthole windows, glass block, and neon. In 1948, it scandalized a visiting Presbyterian minister by opening on Sunday. Less than a decade later, it burned and went down. **39 Celina Street; now a parking lot.**

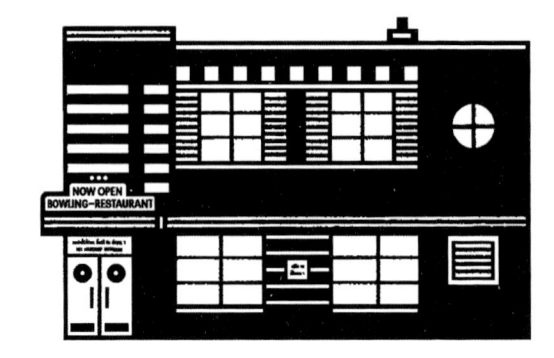

## Westmount Public School 1925-2018

Two storeys of businesslike brick with large, high windows—all the better to bring in light without giving children any views to distract them—that was how the school looked in 1925. By its end, a century later, the school was home to an alternative high school, and outside, the schoolyard to its west had disappeared. The building was on the edge of Oshawa Centre, the mall that had helped dismember Oshawa's downtown. An extension of the mall is planned to replace it. **Pine Avenue west of Westmount Street; now a parking lot.**

## OTTAWA, Ontario

Two hundred years ago, Ottawa was the traditional territory of the Algonquin Anishnaabeg and settlement had not yet begun. Chaudière Falls, a sacred site, was the most prominent feature of this place on the river. After 1826, the building of the Rideau Canal launched Bytown, and its surprising selection as the national capital thirty years later brought waves of capital, building, and architectural skill to the place. The great forces of the twentieth century—suburbanization and automobilization—changed Ottawa but more gently than they did other places. Likewise, the Gréber Plan and other urban renewal efforts had a limited effect on the capital, hitting important buildings in one specific section of downtown. What Ottawa has lost, it has lost to the will of the federal government as well as the ordinary ravages of fire, taste, and time.

---

### Woolworth 1941-1997

In the early twentieth century, Sparks Street was the retail heart of downtown Ottawa. This Woolworth's sat alongside a Kresge's, and Woolworth's claimed to have the longest lunch counter in the country. (Coffee with cream was five cents.) The building was designed by company staff, probably the architect William Sutherland, and presented an art deco stone face to Sparks, and an edgier moderne architecture on Queen Street. When Sparks was converted to a pedestrian mall in 1967, the store remained open. It survived the blows of suburbanization and mall competition to make it until 1987, when Sparks Street construction dealt it a death blow. Scotiabank acquired and demolished both this and the former Kresge's. **172 Sparks Street; now part of the CBC Ottawa Broadcast Centre.**

## Daly Building 1905-1992
Designed by Moses C. Edey. Expanded by Ross & Macdonald, 1913.

Ottawa's first department store was designed by prolific local architect Moses Chamberlain Edey in the Chicago style. A structural grid of iron and steel allowed for open floors; the exterior featured Gloucester limestone and three-light plate-glass windows. Its first tenant was merchant Thomas Lindsay followed by A.E. Rea & Co. The H.J. Daly Co. took it over in 1915, and its name stuck. But the federal government bought the building in 1921 for the new Department of Health, and it remained in government use until 1978. A decade of neglect followed, and it was demolished in 1991. **555 Mackenzie Avenue; now the 700 Sussex Drive condominiums.**

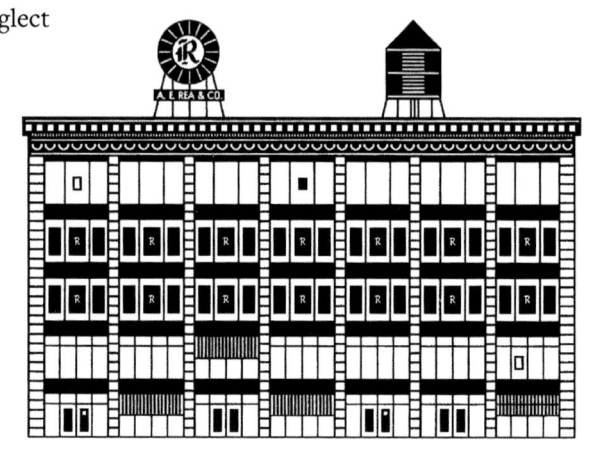

## Green Valley Restaurant 1947-2002

In the 1930s, the rise of the road trip brought about the need for a new building type: the motor hotel, or tourist court. Waldorf Stewart started such a business here on what was the Prescott Highway. Over time the cabins disappeared but the attached restaurant thrived. By 1947 it was serving high tea and Yorkshire pudding in an International Style building, which was much altered but remained open until it burned on New Year's Eve, 2002. **Prince of Wales Drive and Baseline Road.**

## Dominion United Church 1875-1961

Designed by Horsey & Sheard.

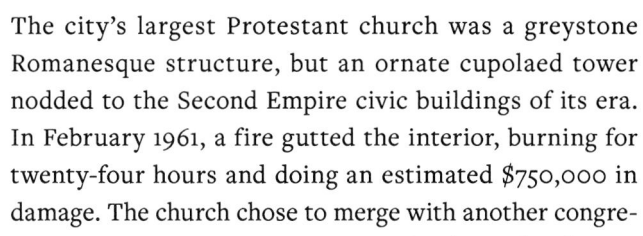

The city's largest Protestant church was a greystone Romanesque structure, but an ornate cupolaed tower nodded to the Second Empire civic buildings of its era. In February 1961, a fire gutted the interior, burning for twenty-four hours and doing an estimated $750,000 in damage. The church chose to merge with another congregation into what is now the Carleton Dominion-Chalmers Centre. The downtown site was redeveloped in 1965, and once again in 1985, as office buildings.

**Queen and O'Connor Streets; now 155 Queen.**

## Garland Building 1898-1969. Designed by Moses C. Edey.

Another Edey structure, this one selling dry goods (in other words, garments and fabrics). The ornate streetfronts employed the sturdy Richardsonian Romanesque styles; later, a Second Empire addition topped it with a steep roof full of rosettes and finials. The building's bones were always modern, however, employing the Kahn system of reinforced concrete. The structure became government offices in 1954.

**Queen and O'Connor Streets; now World Exchange Plaza.**

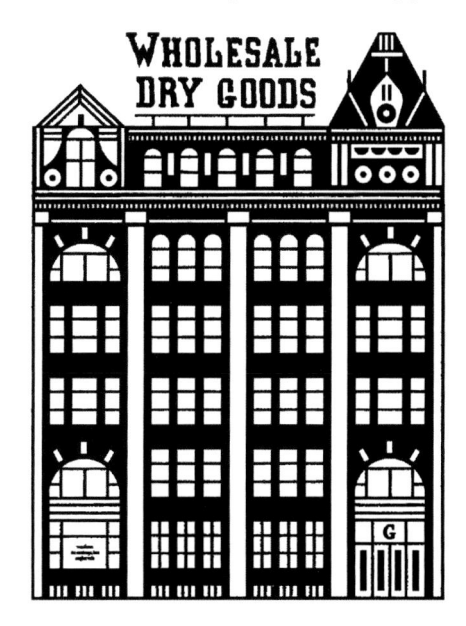

Ontario

## Old Post Office Building
1876-1938. Designed by Walter Chesterton.

A lost sibling to the Parliament Buildings, this post office and customs house faced onto what is now Confederation Square. When it was constructed, however, the Second Empire building faced the Rideau Canal from between two bridges. It stood three symmetrical storeys tall, plus one-and-a-half of attic and one below at the canal. This spot was the focus of twentieth-century efforts to beautify Ottawa and give its centre a more institutional character. In the late 1930s this building was removed, along with City Hall, and was replaced by the Chateau-ish Central Post Office nearby. **Now the National War Memorial.**

---

## Slater House 1880s-1997

A large house in the Queen Anne style, this house survived the transformation of its neighbourhood to make it into the 1990s. It was largely in the hands of one family: engineer Robert Nicholas Slater inherited it from his great-grandfather and lived there until 1920, and his descendants kept it another twenty years before it passed into the control of the Anglican Church. The building—whose architecture strongly recalled the "bay'n'gable" houses of Victorian Toronto—ended up as a church bookstore. The Anglican diocese was arguing to tear it down when the house was damaged by fire in 1992. It was demolished the next year. **412 Sparks Street; now a parking lot.**

## Capitol Cinema 1920-1970

Designed by Thomas W. Lamb.

This was the largest movie theatre in Ottawa, constructed with 2,530 seats as part of the Loews chain. It opened with a mix of vaudeville and film, and hosted the live performances of everyone from Glenn Gould to Jimi Hendrix. Despite its grand architecture—the place had a facade worthy of a Florentine palazzo, and its spacious lobby had a split stair on which to parade—it no longer had a clear role as movie theatres shrunk and the National Arts Centre was going up nearby. It was just fifty years old when it was pulled down. **Southwest corner of Queen and Bank Streets; now an office building.**

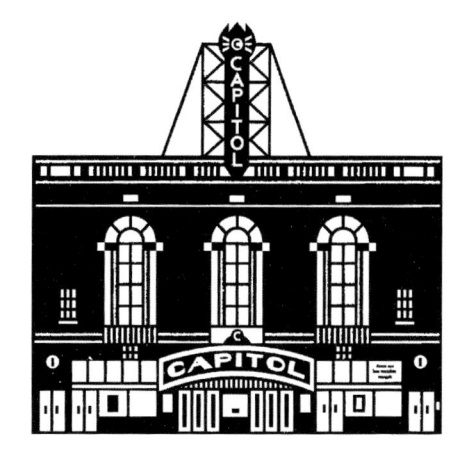

---

## Russell House 1880-1928

Before the Chateau Laurier, there was the Russell: the most important hotel in the capital, and home to Wilfrid Laurier himself for a decade. Reconstructed in 1880 in the Second Empire style, this was the place where, as one regular reportedly wrote, "here argued we affairs of state/How oft' we talked long and late." However, the new Chateau outshone it, and it closed in 1925. The building sat empty until it burned down in 1928, cheered on by spectators who knew it was headed for demolition. The site was cleared as part of the Confederation Square project. **Elgin and Sparks Streets.**

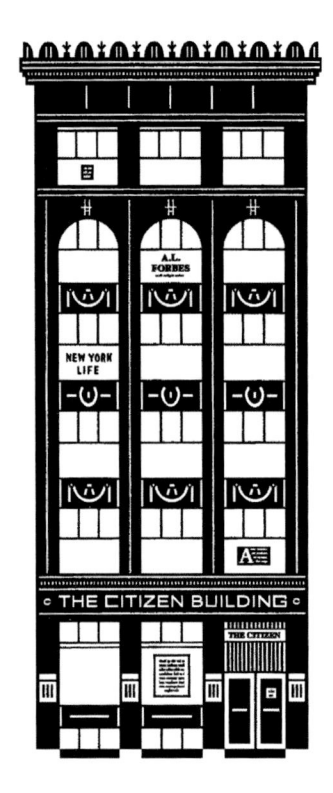

## The Citizen Building 1903-1970s
Designed by Edgar L. Horwood.

Newspapers would often trade on their brands in the field of real estate, and the *Ottawa Citizen* did so with this showy little Edwardian classical structure. It stretched upward six tall storeys, alternating large windows with ornaments of wreaths and garlands before terminating in a cornice of stone flowers. Originally the *Citizen* rented out most of the building to professionals. Later, it took over the entire thing and then built a printing plant around the corner, before leaving the neighbourhood in the 1970s. **136 Sparks Street; now a commercial building.**

## Second City Hall 1877-1931. Designed by Horsey & Sheard.

Ottawa's second city hall reflected the rapid growth of the city in the decades after it became the national capital. Twice the size of its predecessor, this $85,000 building had offices for the mayor, an archive, and city clerks, collectors, and engineers. Horsey & Sheard designed it in the Second Empire style, with a tower that resembled the one on their nearby Dominion Church. The building burned in 1931, and Ottawa's government moved into the Transportation Building at 10 Rideau Street for a quarter-century until its new, modernist city hall was completed. A few years later, the old site was folded into the Confederation Square project. **Now the National Arts Centre.**

**Ottawa Public Library** 1906-1971. Designed by Edgar L. Horwood.

In 1901, the Carnegie Foundation offered Ottawa $100,000 for a free library, and the city set out to build a neoclassical temple of knowledge. (The Royal Society of Canada hoped this would provide an alternative to the "yellow journals" of "socialistic and even atheistic principles" that were being read in town.) Horwood won a design competition for the site, then located in a residential neighbourhood. His architecture had the appropriate character: Corinthian columns flanked the main door, and above it was a stained-glass window featuring Shakespeare, Byron, and at least one Canadian, Archibald Lampman. As the city changed, however, the building had some technical problems, and it was levelled for a brutalist replacement. That building, now, is not long for this world. **120 Metcalfe Street.**

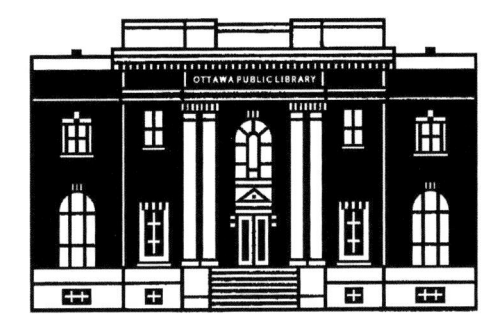

---

**Ottawa Auditorium** 1923-1967. Designed by Richards & Abra.

A purpose-built arena that housed pro hockey and a range of other events from boxing to orchestral music. The first NHL Ottawa Senators team played here from 1923 to 1934; in 1927, they beat the Boston Bruins to win the Stanley Cup on home ice. The Senators surely benefitted from the work of Hermes Proulx, who made them custom hockey sticks from his shop inside the arena. Another home-ice advantage was the weird shape of the rink, which curved into an oval behind each net. **Argyle and O'Connor Streets; now the Taggart Family YMCA.**

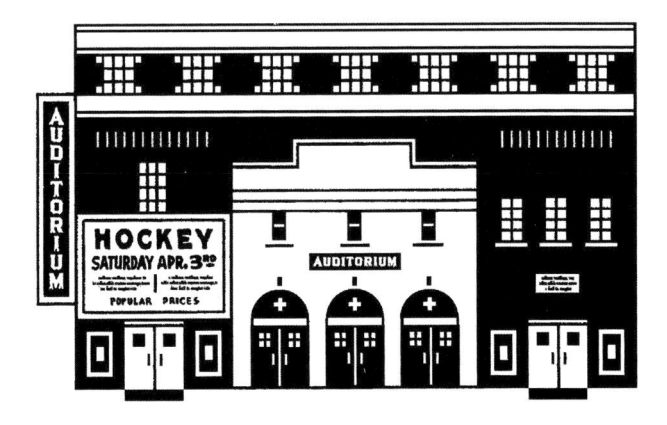

### Central Fire Station 1895-1964. Designed by Moses C. Edey.

Bytown got a volunteer fire department in 1847, and by 1874 it was a professional department with steam engines and five permanent stations. This one, designed by the prolific Edey, was a modestly scaled brick structure whose street facades were dressed up with multihued stonework, corbelling, and a little "boomtown front" that held a keystone. A hotel replaced the station in the 1960s.

**Albert & Lyon Streets; now Delta Ottawa City Centre.**

---

### Sir John Carling Building 1967-2009. Designed by Hart Massey.

The office-tower complement to the experimental farm, this was completed in the centennial year of 1967 to a design by Hart Massey. The architect (whose prominent family also played a major role in Canadian architecture) combined the sleek-box form of an International Style building with the tough textures of brutalism. Each window in the tower was set in a protruding, rectangular concrete frame and capped with textured sunshades. Agriculture Canada staffers enjoyed long views over Dow's Lake and the farm. The building received a heritage designation in 2004, but the government emptied it in 2009 and mostly demolished it in 2014. Its former site is now slated to hold the new Ottawa Civic Hospital.

**930 Carling Avenue.**

**Ontario**

## Cathedral Hall 1958-2012
Designed by Hazelgrove, Lithwick & Lambert.

Anglicanism and modernism did not always fit together, least of all in Ottawa, but this adjunct to Christ Church Cathedral was very much of its time. Its designers (Sid Lithwick was a leading local modernist) drew on the decorative English architecture of the 1950s, fronting the hall with a grid of staggered rectangles and topping the small entrance pavilion with a zoomy curved roof. The church demolished the hall as part of a redevelopment. **420 Sparks Street; now townhouses.**

---

## Grand Union Hotel 1888-1962
Designed by James Mather; extended by Horsey & Sheard.

The very well-located Grand Union sat on Elgin Street, across from City Hall and a short walk from Parliament Hill. The four-and-a-half-storey Second Empire structure was expanded at least once and survived the reconstruction of the area to become government offices. In 1930 it housed offices from three federal departments, but a *Maclean's* writer complained it was falling apart, "a structure of brick, beaverboard and burlap." Its modernist replacement, which flies the Union Jack, is entirely shipshape.
**80 Elgin Street; now the British High Commission Building.**

**Ontario**

# PETERBOROUGH, Ontario

It was once known as the Electric City, for Peterborough was perhaps the first town in the province to establish hydroelectric power. It was early to other things, as well. Its position on the Otonabee River and what became the Trent-Severn Waterway generated industry and trade from the 1850s on and brought engineers and architects to town. Peterborough became a centre for canoe-making and various forms of manufacturing, and a hub for the lumber trade; in the years around 1900 its fortunes rose like a boat in a lift lock. British fashions initially shaped its architecture, and Loyalists brought a strong American influence. Like many Ontario towns, it built with brick and abundant local wood. And it also tore things down.

### Cluxton Building 1881-1973. Designed by John Belcher.

Belcher was an Irish civil engineer who worked on the Trent Canal and for the town of Peterborough. He also practised architecture and designed Peterborough's market hall among dozens of other buildings in town, including Peterborough Collegiate. For William Cluxton, who served as reeve and MP, he designed this commercial block in the Second Empire style, with steep mansard roof and windows capped with an assortment of round and triangular arches.
**George and Hunter Streets; now a bank branch.**

## Bradburn's Opera House 1876-1973
Designed by John Belcher.

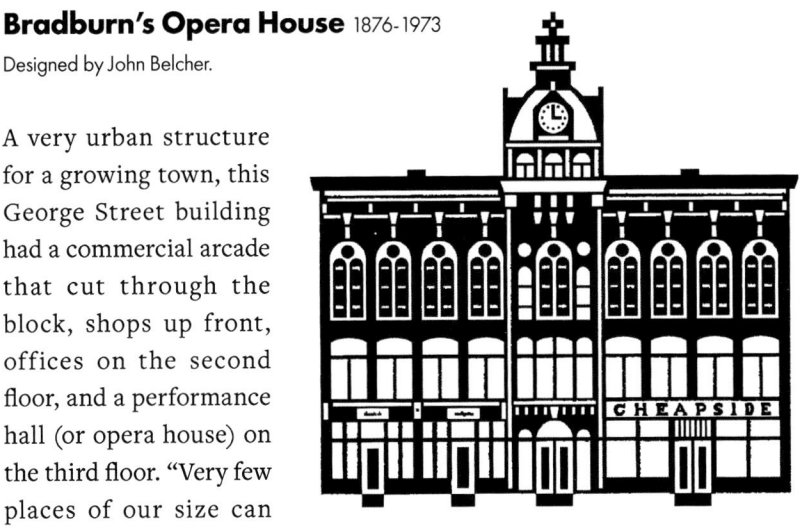

A very urban structure for a growing town, this George Street building had a commercial arcade that cut through the block, shops up front, offices on the second floor, and a performance hall (or opera house) on the third floor. "Very few places of our size can boast of such a well-appointed amusement hall," claimed a city directory in 1884. The larger Grand Opera House captured many travelling shows after 1905, but this room survived. At the end of the 1960s, plans for the Peterborough Square mall saw most of its block demolished in a "renewal" project supported by the province. This was Peterborough's worst instance of heritage destruction. **338 George Street; now Peterborough Square.**

---

## St. Paul's Presbyterian Church 1840s-2020
Rebuilt by Gordon & Helliwell, 1884.

Facing onto Victoria Park, this church was designed in a severe Ontario Gothic style, with red brick almost from top to bottom and barely a hint of stone. On the back, however, was an ornate and playful rotunda. The church's end was a familiar story: the congregation was shrinking, the main sanctuary was in serious disrepair, and the developer who bought the place viewed it as too expensive to repair and retain.
**Murray and Water Streets.**

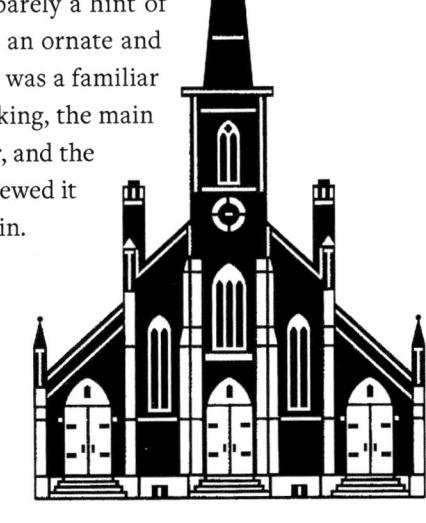

# SARNIA, Ontario

Settled after the War of 1812, Sarnia grew with the flow of oil. The first commercial oil well in North America was established in Oil Springs, forty kilometres away, in 1858. This was the seed for an entire industry that, along with lake shipping and sawmills, powered the economy. The result was a relatively dense city with a finely textured Victorian downtown. In 1953, a huge tornado tore through Sarnia, damaging or destroying much of the city fabric. The result was a patchwork of repairs and empty lots, which was stretched and torn by aggressive urban renewal efforts in the decades to follow. In an attempt to bring the city up to date, midcentury Sarnia doubled down on a shopping mall. The results, architecturally and economically, were tough on the city.

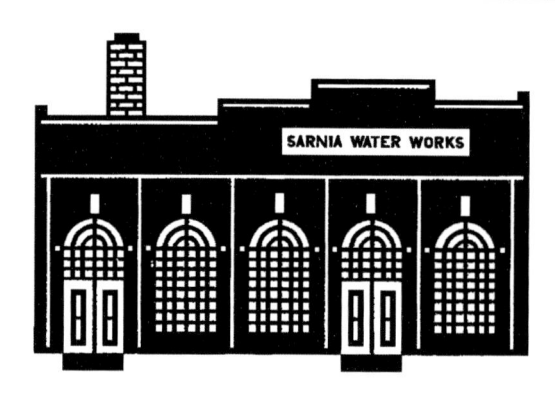

## Sarnia Water Works 1913-1970s

Right up into the 1870s, the people of Sarnia got their water straight from the St. Clair River. Local workers would fill their wagons and cruise through town; individual citizens would fill their own buckets. Outbreaks of waterborne disease prompted a push for a civic waterworks, which was first completed in 1875. This brick structure stood near the mouth of the river for many years until its much larger replacement was constructed nearby. **Now Waterfront Park.**

## Sarnia City Hall 1876-1954

The sign over the front door read WELCOME. This high-Victorian city hall, made of red brick with round-arched windows, white stone quoining, and a bell tower, anchored a block in the central business district. It survived the 1953 tornado, only to be demolished the following year for an expanded Hudson's Bay store. That, in turn, was demolished to make way for the shopping mall that ate downtown.
**Now Bayside Centre (closed).**

## Armouries Building 1893-1962. Designed by Henry G. Phillips.

Following the twin disruptions of the tornado and urban renewal, city government went looking for a new permanent home. The chosen spot was the site of this building. It had been designed in the Romanesque style for a youth-development organization called the Boys' Brigade, then became a movie theatre before the federal government purchased it for an armoury. The city took control and levelled it; the new civic building, in the International Style, was completed a few years later.
**Front and George Streets.**

# SUDBURY, Ontario

Sudbury and nickel are fused together. While this was the territory of the Atikameksheng Anishnawbek, who traded furs with the French, the city as such didn't exist until the 1880s. First the CPR arrived, establishing a log-cabin company town. Within a few years prospectors picked up on the unusual, meteor-smashed geology of the place—the Anishinaabe had mined copper here—and the trajectory of the mining city was set. Log cabins gave way to masonry after a brick factory was built in 1902, and a succession of early-twentieth-century booms brought more permanent structures. Mining ravaged the local environment, and the forces of mall and sprawl took a toll on downtown in the later twentieth century. The city is bent on bringing life back to its core.

---

## Cochrane Block 1893-1974

Early Sudbury, said Frank Cochrane, was a place where "no building was more than two storeys high." Cochrane pushed back against that tradition with this, a three-storey building that housed his prosperous hardware store and other tenants. Cochrane himself became mayor and then MPP, and Cochrane-Dunlop Hardware became a chain that spanned the province until the 1980s. In Sudbury, it would move into a bigger building before long.
**Cedar and Durham Streets; now the Scotiabank building.**

## Nickel Range Hotel

1914-1976

Designed by Henry W. Angus.

A boomtime build on Elgin, which then was packed with hotels, bars, and restaurants. North Bay architect Angus provided a solid Edwardian classical building; the front door featured an ornate canopy and there were Doric columns in the lobby, but the rooms upstairs had low ceilings. In the 1940s, a Ukrainian immigrant named George Trebek worked here as a pastry chef; his son Alex got a job as a bellhop and learned some life lessons. **Elm Street near Elgin Street; now a Shoppers Drug Mart.**

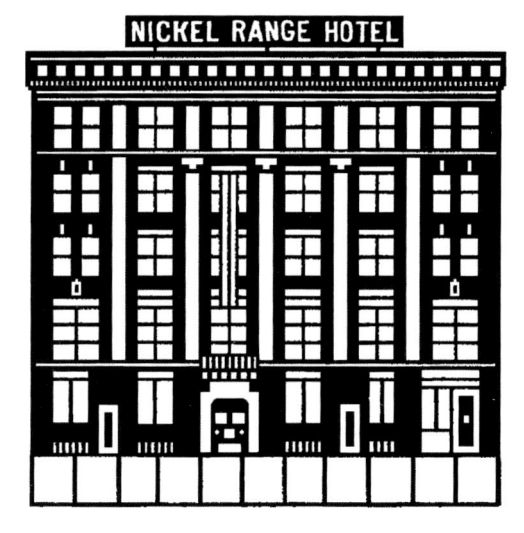

---

## Federal Building & Post Office 1915-1959. Designed by David Ewart.

One of the few stone buildings in town, this was designed before the First World War and completed as a wartime boom reached the city (nickel was used for armour plating). The federal Department of Public Works gave the pentagonal, ashlar-stone structure a ninety-foot clock tower, which provided a ceremonial centre to the town; a local watchmaker built the clock. The building was torn down for a commercial building that then held a Woolworth's, which in turn was demolished for a parking lot.

**Durham and Elm Streets.**

**Ontario**

# TORONTO, Ontario

Toronto has always been a place of exchange. Even its name originates elsewhere: it was a Kanien'kéha (Mohawk) name for Lake Simcoe and travelled south through the confusion of French and British colonists. The city's architecture has also been borrowed, starting with the Castle Frank that John Graves Simcoe built out of logs for himself and his wife, Elizabeth. In the three hundred years since the place was settled, it has grown dramatically and at increasing speed: a trading post, then a brick Georgian village, then a Victorian industrial centre that, in turn, sprawled into a modern, diverse metropolis. All these changes have left much of the city intact, but they have also wiped out buildings of every era, right up to the space age.

**Bata Building** 1964-2007. Designed by John B. Parkin & Associates.

This temple to shoes occupied a prominent hilltop site in Don Mills, a modernist planned neighbourhood. The Bata company turned to the Parkin architecture firm, leading modernists, who designed an elegant concrete box perched on a field of splayed "umbrella" columns. The lead designer John C. Parkin (who worked with the unrelated John B. Parkin) created an interior lined with rosewood and stacked with furniture by Eames and Saarinen. Chairs and building were discarded forty years later, for what is at least a worthy replacement: the Aga Khan Museum and its accompanying garden. **59 Wynford Drive.**

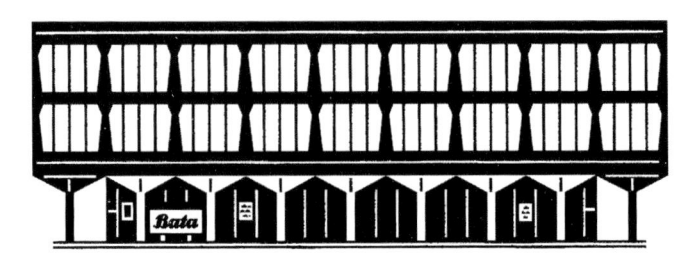

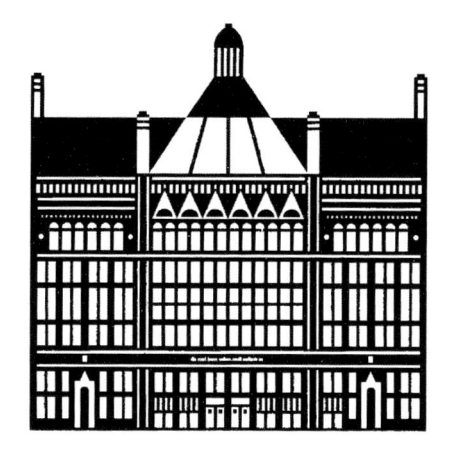

## Board of Trade Building

1891-1958. Designed by James & James.

The Toronto Board of Trade held an international design competition for this showpiece of a building. (They had recently merged with the Toronto Corn Exchange.) The English architects delivered a round-cornered fantasy topped with arches-in-gables, a steeply sloped tower, and a cupola. The architecture was a close copy of a Boston building, which suited Toronto businessmen of the time; its construction went far over budget, which did not. The Toronto Transit Commisssion took over the building for more than thirty years, then it was wrecked for a parking lot. **Northeast corner of Front and Yonge Streets; now an office building.**

## Temple Building 1897-1970

Designed by G.W. Gouinlock.

Once, ten storeys was enough to tower over downtown Toronto. At Bay and Richmond Streets, the Temple's brick and sandstone bookended a low crowd of houses and warehouses. It was framed in state-of-the art steel, and its Richardsonian walls of heavy masonry advertised the solidity of the building and of the Independent Order of Foresters. That mutual-aid society was led in Canada by Dr. Oronhyatekha, a Mohawk who was among the first Indigenous people to receive a Canadian medical degree. The building included a museum housing his collection of artifacts, including wampum belts and a Burmese gong. **310 Bay Street; now a new office building.**

**Ontario**

## Shell Tower 1955-1985
Designed by George Robb.

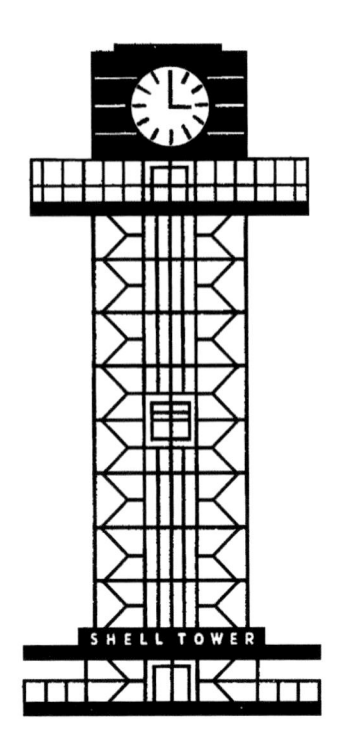

An exhibition is a place to see what's new, and when this ninety-foot observation tower opened at the Canadian National Exhibition in 1955, it was very much of the moment. Robb, a local architect and professor, brought together several devices of modernist architecture that were unfamiliar to the architecturally conservative city: an exposed steel frame, large expanses of backlit glass, and carefully stripped-back details—accented in Shell Oil's trademark red. From a distance, its analog clock was a landmark for the fair; from up top, you could rest your hands on a teak railing and look out across the growing city.
**Exhibition Place.**

---

## Registry of Deeds & Land Titles Building 1917-1960
Designed by Charles S. Cobb.

A trace of Toronto's big plans. In the 1910s, the architect John Lyle led an effort to create a new civic complex in the fashion of the Beaux-Arts movement. The first piece was the registry. The neoclassical pomp of Cobb's architecture won a design competition, and it was built with French and Italian marble. But the civic centre stalled, and the registry office was left overlooking the immigrant quarters of St. John's Ward. Half a century later, the area was levelled for a new city hall. As that curving concrete hall rose, the registry's stone came down.

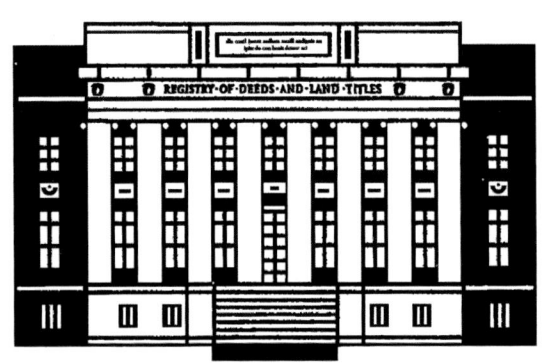

**361 University Avenue; now the Ontario Superior Court of Justice.**

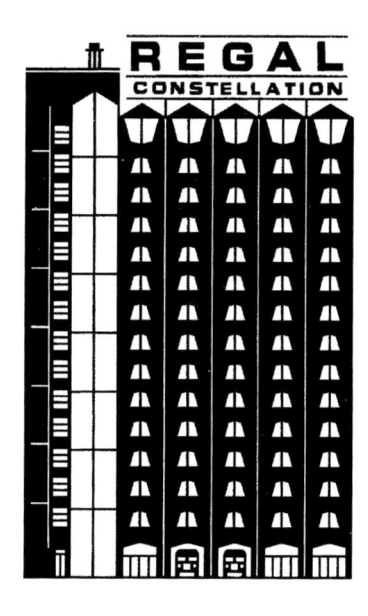

## Regal Constellation Hotel
1962-2011

One tower designed by Webb Zerafa Menkes.

As you prepared to launch into the skies, why not stay at the Constellation? The hotel served the brand new Aeroquay at Toronto's airport, and as air travel grew it expanded into a convention centre and two-tower complex. On the airport side, a tented facade and six-sided windows brought a jet age sparkle to the place. (Some things were old-fashioned: its longtime proprietor, George Kalmar, lived up on the fifteenth floor.) The hotel saw its fortunes suffer with the SARS outbreak in 2003, then stood half-demolished for years, a relic of an era that already seemed far away. **900 Dixon Road; now a parking lot.**

## Honest Ed's
1943-2018

"There's no place like this place, anyplace!" This was one of the slogans the discount retailer Honest Ed Mirvish cooked up and displayed at his Toronto store, which delivered bargains to the city's working class. Over time, the Mirvish family expanded their businesses from a small shopfront to two city blocks. The store became a sprawling maze of bins, pillars, mirrored walls, obscure housewares, and hand-painted signs with corny slogans. The place was defined by its signs, the biggest of which (built in 1984) incorporated thousands of light bulbs into a Vegas-like display. Demolition revealed the bones of the place, a haphazard set of ad-hoc add-ons that somehow stood up for seventy years. **581 Bloor Street West; now Mirvish Village.**

**Odeon Carlton** 1948-1974
Designed by Jay I. English.

With 2,300 seats, the Odeon chain's showcase theatre was the grandest cinema-going experience in town. Odeon architect Jay English (who had worked on the Empire State Building) designed its interior in flashy deco style: a stylized mural depicted film production. The building's white exterior spoke the language of high modernism, including strip windows and a rectangular tower that could be seen for blocks. Sadly, the building had bad timing. It opened (with *Oliver Twist* starring Alec Guinness) just as television began to steal viewers from large cinemas. By the seventies, the Odeon went dark. **20 Carlton Street.**

---

**Shea's Hippodrome** 1914-1957. Designed by Leon Lempert & Son.

A hippodrome was a stadium for chariot races in Ancient Greece. Here, instead of horses, three thousand Torontonians could see vaudeville stars, then the "talkies" — mass entertainment from the Ziegfields to Elvis. The architects, from Buffalo, New York, designed one of the city's most grandiloquent structures: a Byzantine-deco extravaganza, its front facade of white brick and terracotta capped by copper-domed towers. After they fell, city hall's two new towers rose on this site. **440 Bay Street; now Nathan Phillips Square.**

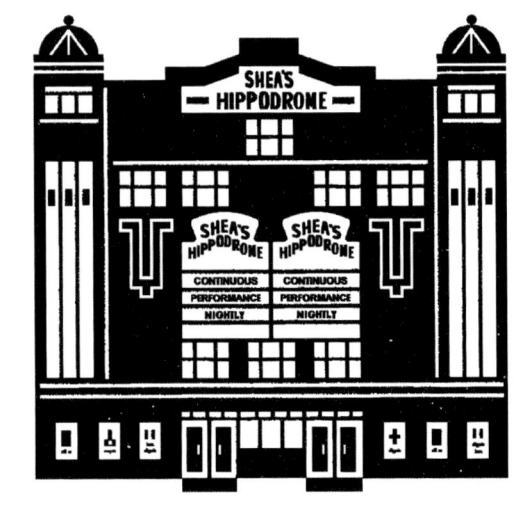

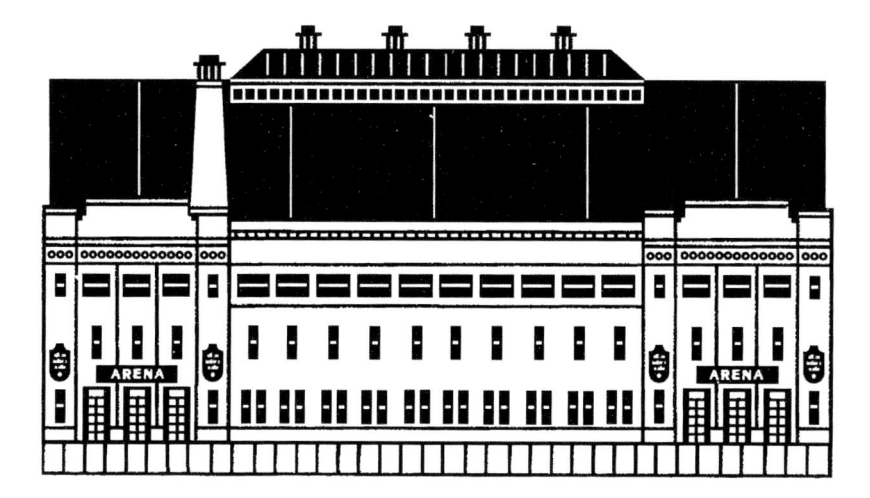

**Arena Gardens** 1912-1989. Designed by Ross & Macfarlane with F.H. Herbert.

It opened with opera, a performance led by violinist Nahan Franko of New York's Metropolitan Opera with a host of singers, but this big, steel-framed shed would be better known for hockey. Its owners, including Casa Loma owner Sir Henry Pellatt, created an artificial ice surface here and soon acquired the city's new National Hockey League franchise. That team would become the St. Patricks and then the Maple Leafs. The Leafs moved to their new home in 1931, bringing the word *gardens* and operatic highs and lows with them. The arena would host concerts, conventions, curling, and roller skating until its end. **68 Mutual Street; now housing and Arena Gardens Park.**

**O'Keefe Brewery** 1892-1965. Designed by August Maritzen with Smith & Gemmell.

Industrial Toronto was fuelled by beer. Eugene O'Keefe was among the first to make this a big business, and in the 1890s his company called on the Chicago brewery specialist Maritzen to create a castle of malt and hops. Concrete floors and a steel-and-iron structure kept away fire; facades of arched brick and Second Empire-styled tower loomed over the spire of the Catholic church across the street. **11 Gould Street; now part of 10 Dundas East.**

---

**Wyld, Grasett & Darling Building** 1886-1904. Designed by David B. Dick.

On the cold night of April 19, 1904, a watchman on Wellington Street sounded the alarm: fire! The flames spread quickly across the warehouses and shops of Toronto's downtown, eating up a wave of buildings designed to show off the city's growing commercial strength. The dry-goods wholesalers of Wyld, Grasett & Darling had hired prominent local architect Dick for their corner emporium. Two weeks later, when the last flames were put out, Dick's facades of red brick and rusticated stone still stood; the wooden structure behind it, together with a treasure of textiles and groceries, had gone up in smoke. **Wellington and Bay Streets; now Brookfield Place.**

**Ontario**

## Sam the Record Man
1961-2010

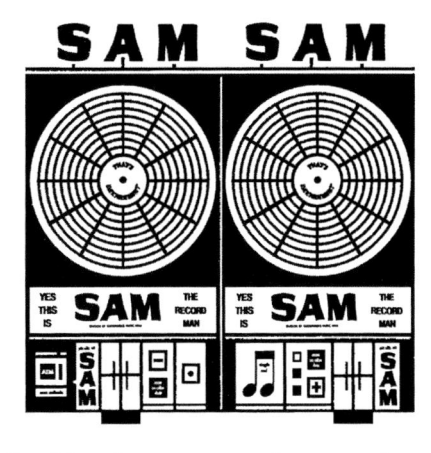

Somewhere under the piles of records, and, later, tapes and CDs; somewhere under the racks, bins, signs, and autographed memorabilia; somewhere was a building. But Sam the Record Man's flagship store was all about the music. Long before streaming, its chaotic interior offered routes into new musical worlds. Visually, it was defined by the two neon signs — spinning records — that occupied its front facade. These were saved when the store went bust, and years later they reappeared around the corner, a dozen floors up on top of a building. **347-349 Yonge Street; now the Ryerson University Student Learning Centre.**

---

## Second Union Station 1873-1927. Designed by E.P. Hannaford.

The railways brought wealth to Toronto in the mid-nineteenth century, but they also brought competing stations and tracks that sprawled across the city's central waterfront. The Grand Trunk Railway built this one of yellow brick, with three mansard-roofed towers to the south and a huge skylit shed to the north. (This meant that, once you left a train, you had to cross the tracks to get into the city, but it looked impressive from the lake.) The complex grew bigger and dirtier, until the current Union Station was built, and all the city's rail traffic ended up in one place. **South of Station Street, west of York Street; now the Skywalk and rail tracks.**

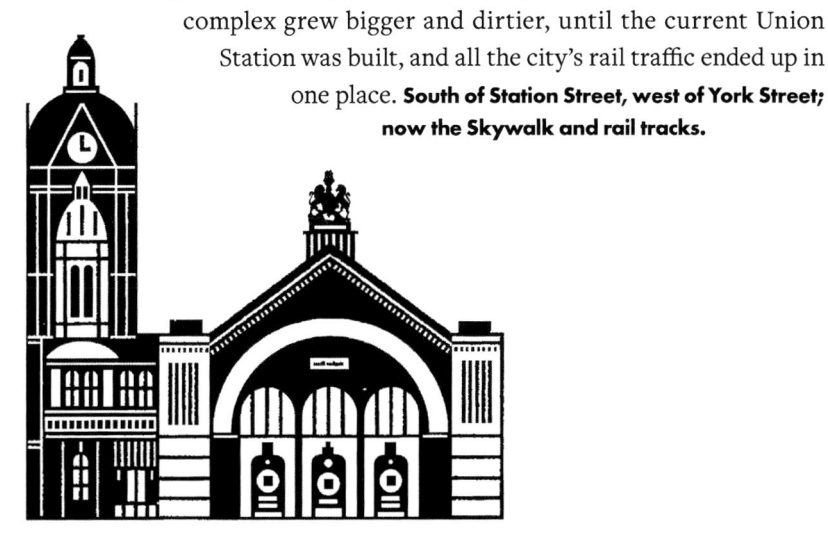

## Walnut Hall 1856-2007. Designed by John Tully.

When the local politician John O'Donohoe built this row of upscale houses, he couldn't have imagined what would become of them. The posh neighbourhood soon went downscale, and the houses became rooming houses and a hotel. One was converted into a storefront. But the buildings survived in this altered form, long enough to become rare relics of Georgian Toronto. Known as Walnut Hall, they sat empty and crumbling from the 1980s until, one night, they began to fall down. **102-108 Shuter Street; now a residential building.**

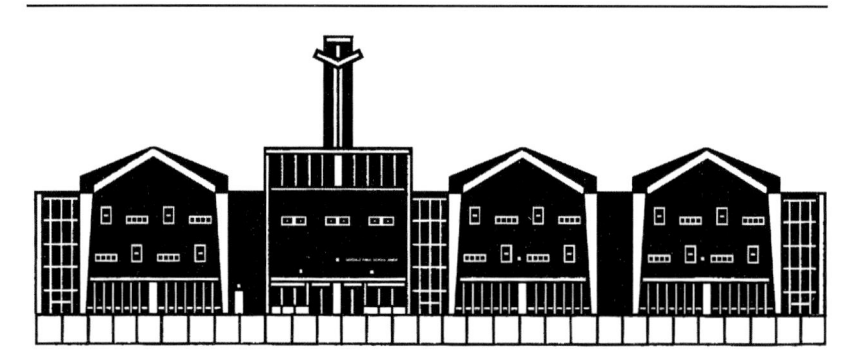

## Davisville Junior Public School 1962-2018

Designed by Peter Pennington and Toronto Board of Education staff.

In Toronto, the postwar school boom brought radical modernism into the city's staid neighbourhoods. Here, the Mancunian architect Peter Pennington imported a pointy and playful idiom inspired by the 1951 Festival of Britain. The building felt like a group of pavilions, each comfortably scaled for a community of students and topped with an irregular paraboloid roof. Since the building housed the city's first school specifically for Deaf students, an intercom system employed a set of colour-coded lights. Pennington brought triangle motifs to door handles, radiator grilles, and coat hooks, giving the place a uniform space-age cheer. It was fun while it lasted. **43 Millwood Road; now a new school.**

**Trinity College** 1851-1956. Designed by Kivas Tully.

Here was an Anglican fortress brought low. John Strachan, Toronto's much-feared bishop, created the college when the city's main university turned secular. He chose a site well outside Toronto's limits and far from its temptations; Tully delivered an appropriately stern and spiky architecture. In the 1920s, the college moved uptown to merge back into the University of Toronto, in a near-replica (which still stands) of its previous building. Back on Queen Street, a pair of ornate gates remain, now framing Trinity-Bellwoods Park, where what happens on a summer afternoon would scandalize the bishop. **Queen Street West at Strachan Avenue.**

---

**Toronto Star Building** 1929-1972
Designed by Chapman & Oxley.

Superman's Toronto office was on King Street. As a kid, Joe Shuster hawked the *Toronto Star*. When he and Jerry Siegel created the Man of Steel in the 1930s, they modelled Clark Kent's newspaper, the *Daily Planet*, after the *Star*, and its building after this ornate blond-brick deco headquarters. This was where reporters and editors toiled, ads were sold, and papers were printed. A team of wall-washers worked to cleanse the place of ink dust. In the 1960s, a new wave of big bank headquarters remade King and Bay, pushing the paper to the waterfront. **80 King Street West; now First Canadian Place.**

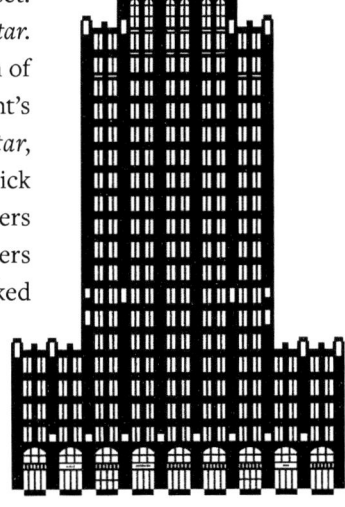

**Ontario**

**The Armouries** 1891-1963. Designed by Thomas Fuller.

Like federal armouries across the country, this giant building had the air of a medieval castle: towers capped with battlements stood at its four corners. Inside, a very modern steel structure spanned a vast hall. This was the work of the federal government's chief architect, at a moment when the state was constructing grand public buildings across the country. In Toronto, this was selected as the site of a new courthouse, prompting one of the first major preservation battles in the city. A local alderman called the armoury an "ugly duckling," and that point of view won out. **University Avenue at Albert Street; now the Ontario Superior Court of Justice.**

# WINDSOR, Ontario

Canada's southernmost city, Windsor has long been shaped by its connection to the border. Its colonial origins begin with Sandwich, established to welcome Loyalists from Detroit after the American Revolution; later, Black Americans escaped here along the Underground Railroad, many of them settling in the area. But the rise of the car, after 1905, remade Detroit and also Windsor. "Ford City" grew up in the 1910s and evolved into East Windsor, eventually evolving along with Sandwich into Windsor. The car pulled some energy away from the region's core, which also suffered when auto booms turned to busts. What's been lost along the way includes public buildings, watering holes, and auto architecture.

---

**Municipal Courts Building** 1950s-2000s. Designed by Sheppard & Masson.

In 1903, Windsor took over a former school—which had been a segregated school for Black students—as a city hall. The 1950s brought a much more intentional approach: the city followed the modernist urban design fashions of the day to demolish several blocks and build a new civic square, with public buildings scattered around irregular plazas. Not much was realized. However, the city's leading architecture firm did create a new city hall and this nearby. Where city hall had a firmly vertical stone tower and blue tile, the courthouse had stone-framed rectangular windows and glass block, though it shared the same mix of orange brick. A complementary pair, both are now gone.

**City Hall Square South.**

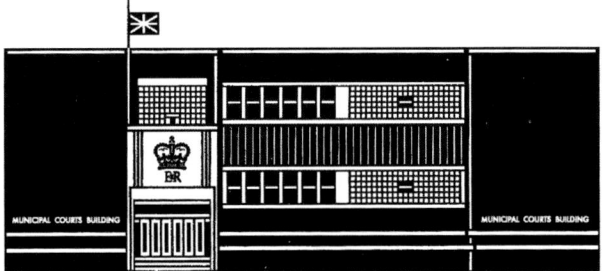

## Bridge Tavern
1904-2017

When the United States introduced Prohibition in 1920, Windsor was infused with alcohol headed across the border by speedboat or a drive over the ice. It was also flooded with drinkers from Detroit who came to Canada to partake. The Bridge, as it became known, was part of that history and remained for over a century as a low-key student-friendly bar in the West End. It closed in 2007 and stood closed until 2016, when the city took it over for unpaid taxes and demolished it. **1886 University Avenue West.**

---

## Easton Edwards Building 1929-1970s. Designed by Cameron & Ralston.

A deco palace of the automobile, this three-storey car dealership and service centre captured the energy of 1920s Windsor. A plate-glass bay window connected the street with the showroom, where the terrazzo floors and concrete structure bore pastel colours. Speaking of the front facade, a local newspaper praised the "Moorish and Byzantine architecture which has as of late branched out as 'modernistic.'" The architects also designed the landmark William C. Kennedy Collegiate, though here it was probably the younger partner, William Ralston, who brought the forward-looking architecture. **567 Goyeau Street.**

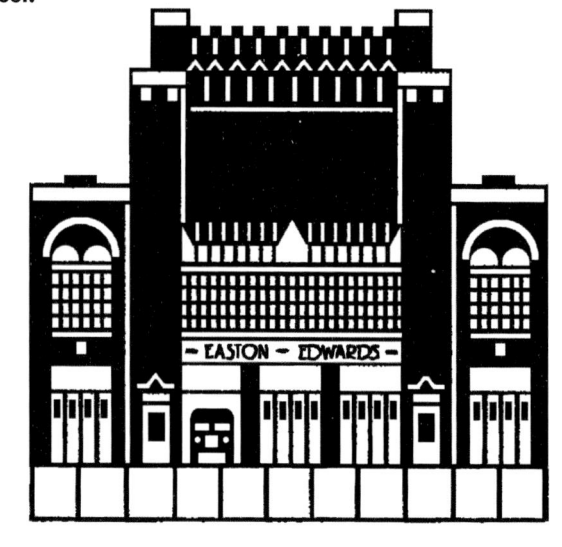

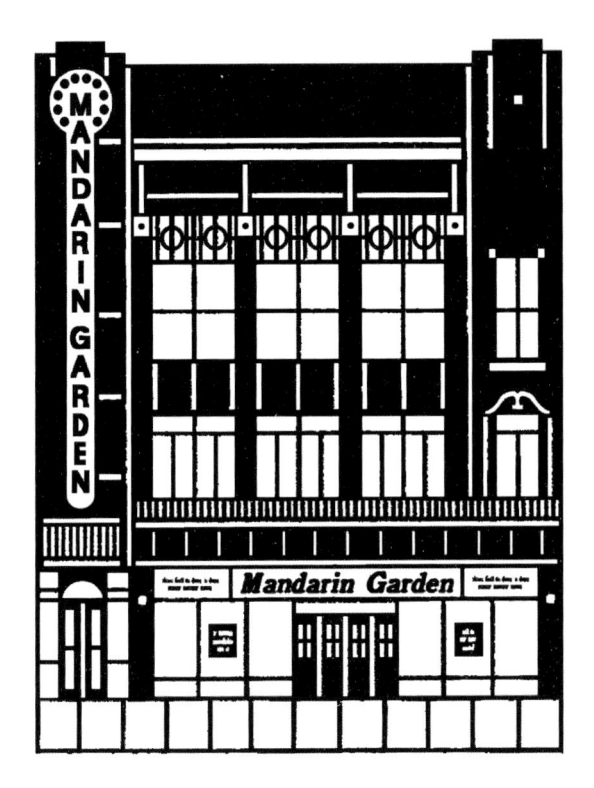

**Mandarin Garden** 1927-1933. Designed by Jacques & Allaster.

Billed as "Windsor's finest café," this local landmark was founded by a group of Chinese-Canadian restaurateurs named in the local newspaper as the Gan Brothers. In the 1920s they took a two-floor space in a commercial building and hired local architects to redesign the place: outside, a second-floor wrought-iron balcony and limestone panels; inside, a dance floor and lacquered furniture. Their newspaper advertisements trumpeted prix-fixe menus and private radio broadcasts of playoff hockey games. The space was, apparently, "an Oriental dream of loveliness, luxurious in appointments." Perhaps too luxurious; the architect Andrew Allaster sued for unpaid fees and won a court case in 1933, helping, along with the Depression, to bring the Garden down. **Ouelette Avenue near University Avenue.**

# WINNIPEG, Manitoba

The gateway to the West, breadbasket of the British Empire, boomtown. This was Winnipeg in the early twentieth century, as waves of migrants chased free land and prairie soil. The arrival of railways in the 1880s made the city the commercial and shipping centre of the region, and it grew accordingly from 42,000 people in 1901 to 160,000 in 1916. New arrivals saw a downtown where the railways, banks, and merchants created showpieces of brick, steel, and local Tyndall stone. Top architects from Toronto and New York were employed to attract both visitors and the capital flowing out of grain and oil. Of course, this seemingly endless growth came to an end, and many architectural traces of the boom years fell to postwar ideas of progress that levelled much of the downtown. The Exchange District largely survives, but the rich, ambitious architecture created by the first two generations of settlers is largely lost.

**Coronation Block** 1883-2012. Originally designed by Victor Stewart.

Built in 1883, this structure served as a civic headquarters for a few years while the second city hall was built. Soon afterward, a Chinese community established itself downtown, and this building became its hub. The main floor housed first the Nanking Chop Suey House and then Shanghai Restaurant, run by the Lee family all the way from 1941 to 2011. Later renovations and expansion gave the place a modern flair—turquoise booths and tile mosaics depicting Chinese pagodas—that remained untouched until it closed and was demolished. **238 King Street; now a vacant lot.**

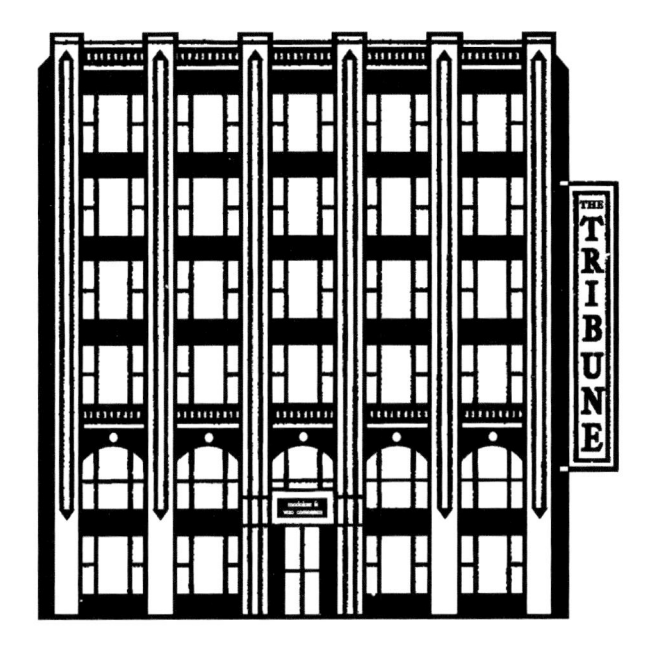

**Tribune Building** 1914-1983. Designed by John D. Atkinson.

This Chicago Style loft building was a palace of newsprint. The *Tribune* was an important local newspaper for most of the twentieth century, and the architecture of its headquarters reflected this work. The facades supported twenty-eight newspaper-themed gargoyles made in Chicago: a printer with his tools, an editor with his scissors. In 1969 precast concrete replaced the terracotta cladding, and the gargoyles came down; two survive in the collection of the Manitoba Museum. The *Tribune* went under in 1980, and the building went down soon afterward. **257 Smith Street; now a parking lot.**

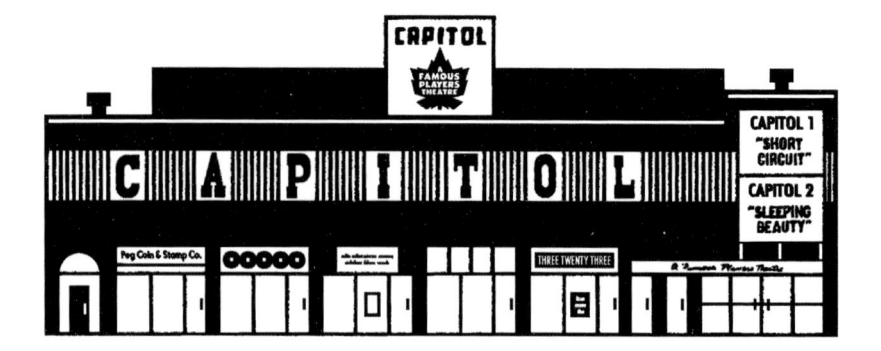

**Capitol Theatre** 1921-2003. Designed by Thomas W. Lamb.

The Famous Players Canadian Corporation was battling for control of the cinema business in the 1920s, and in Winnipeg it went big. With 2,200 seats, this was the largest single-screen movie theatre ever built in Winnipeg. Its architect, Lamb, designed grand and grandly decorated movie palaces in New York and across North America. Here he designed a two-part structure: moviegoers entered on Portage Avenue and crossed a bridge to the huge, gilded auditorium behind on Donald Street, passing between dramatic cove lights and plaster textured to look like marble. The theatre was split into two separate rooms in 1979, and like many of its grand siblings, it did not survive. **313 Donald Street; now a plaza.**

---

**Regent Theatre** 1913-2008
Designed by Alexander D. Melville.

The Regent was a movie palace that packed 850 patrons into a long, narrow, barrel-vaulted auditorium. Out front, an arched facade (of a type known as a Coney Island front) declared the showiness of the place with flashing lights and, once upon a time, stucco reliefs of trumpet-playing cherubs. Later it became an adult theatre called the Epic and a centre for the homeless.
**646 Main Street; now the Winnipeg Regional Health Authority.**

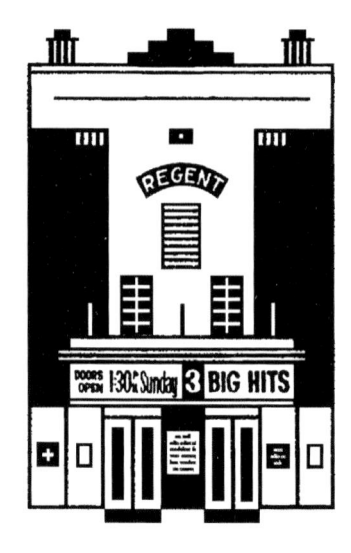

## Manitoba College 1882-1964
Designed by Barber & Barber.

An imposing polychrome pile, Manitoba College featured towers pointed and flat-topped (with hints of the Moorish and the Gothic) piercing its red-and-grey stone walls and mansard roof. Fittingly, then, the building changed Christian denominations. Originally constructed for the Protestant Manitoba College, it was taken over by the Catholic St. Paul's College in 1931. The two schools merged into larger institutions, and the college campus was replaced, for many years, by a parking lot. **435 Ellice Avenue; now offices of National Research Council Canada.**

---

## Fire Hall No. 2 1882-1941
Designed by Smith & Bruce.

In the 1870s, Winnipeg was growing fast and had need of a firefighting service. A volunteer fire brigade was recognized in 1877, and three fire halls were built soon after, all handsome civic buildings with neoclassical flair. Unfortunately, these had no heating, lighting, or indoor plumbing, and firefighters slept in one giant room with the horses nearby. Prominent local architects Daniel Smith and William Bruce rebuilt the place during a wave of fire hall construction around the city. The horses were replaced by trucks in the 1930s, and this hall fell soon after.
**Smith Street and York Avenue; now the 160 Smith Street tower.**

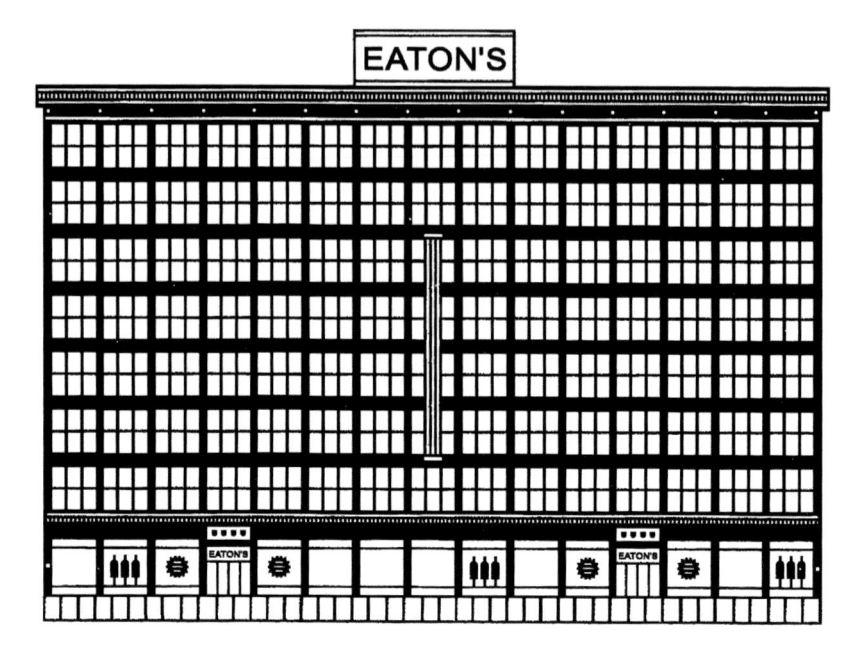

**Eaton's Department Store** 1905-2002. Designed by John Woodman.

The biggest building in downtown Winnipeg when it opened, this store's five storeys of Chicago-style steel and cast iron spanned almost an entire block. (Horizontal bands of brick and white stone hinted toward the abstraction that would come with modernist architecture.) The first Eaton's outside of Toronto, it was expanded in 1907, 1908, and 1912, growing with the fortunes of the middle classes and of Winnipeg. People came to shop, to rest in the fourth-floor lounge, or to have a grand lunch at the Grill Room or a sandwich in the cafeteria. Up to eight thousand people worked here at a time. The store closed entirely with the Eaton's chain in 1999 and, after much debate, was completely demolished. **320 Portage; now the MTS Centre.**

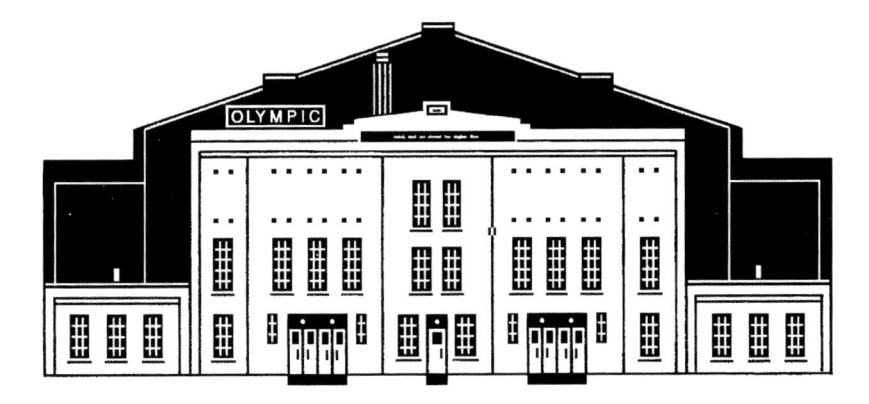

**Olympic Rink** 1923-1968. Designed by Frank Robert Evans.

A social centre of the North End, this place hosted "dog shows, flower shows, political and religious gatherings, boxing and wrestling cards and box lacrosse," as a newspaper story put it—plus youth hockey, though the ice for the first thirty years was maintained without refrigeration equipment. In October 1935, hundreds of locals crowded in to hear the first Jewish cabinet member in Canada speak in a political campaign. Later the building housed the North End's junior hockey team, the Warriors. It became a curling rink and was replaced by "North Winnipeg's first high-rise apartment building," which took its name.
**480 Charles Street; now Olympic Towers.**

## Ogilvie Flour Mill
1881-2005

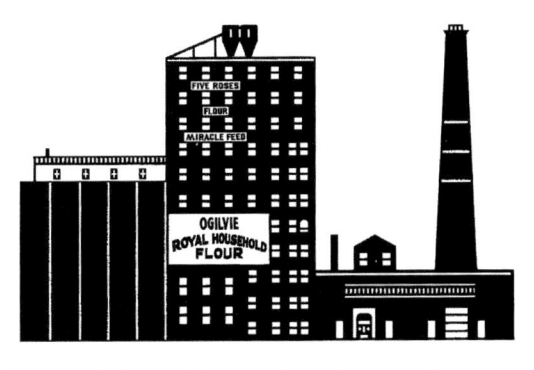

Manitoba's prairies were an ideal place to grow red fife wheat, and red fife was milled into flour at this massive complex. Montréal's Ogilvie Co. arrived early in the red fife era and chose this spot in Point Douglas near the Red River's water and the CPR's main line. By 1900 Ogilvie milled three thousand barrels a day. The six-storey mill marked a transition in Winnipeg's economy, and it was joined by an eleven-storey elevator and a host of other buildings. Ogilvie had fallen prey to bigger American competitors by 1990, and the complex was taken down with 325 kilograms of TNT. **53-55 Higgins Avenue.**

**Manitoba**

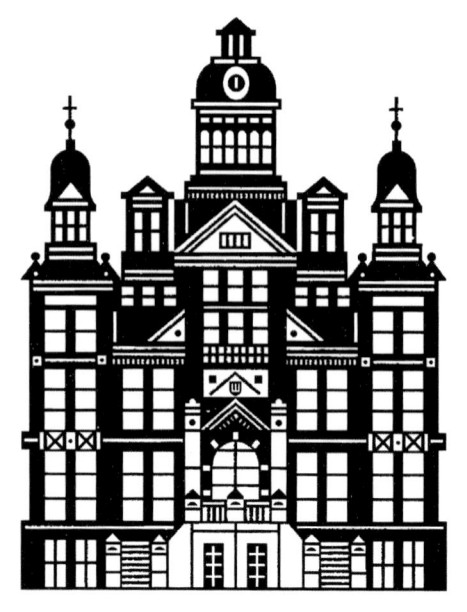

## Second City Hall 1886-1962
Designed by Barber & Barber.

Known as the Gingerbread House, this wildly eclectic pile captured the gangly ambition of the booming city. It rose through four storeys of striped brick and stone before dissolving into a crowd of gables and turrets, a Victorian frippery that hardly fit into the rigid industrial grid of downtown. The building was constructed in controversy—some claimed it was too big and too expensive and that the architects were overpaid—but it outlasted many changes until the early 1960s. By then a drafty hulk (with a goat skeleton, somehow, in the attic), it came down for another city hall designed by locals.

**510 Main Street; now Winnipeg Civic Centre.**

---

## Post Office and Customs Office 1886-1962
Designed by Thomas Fuller.

The federal government's chief architect Thomas Fuller designed this, Winnipeg's fifth post office, with some flair: its brick and ornately carved stone rose four tall storeys, culminating in rounded arches and fearsome parapets. A new post office was built a decade later, and this became the city's customs building and then an extension of the Wheat Board, before the mass demolitions of the 1960s took it down.

**401 Main Street at McDermot; now the Canadian Wheat Board Building.**

**Market Building** 1889-1964
Designed by George Creeford Browne.

Initially, this was the city's source for food of all kinds. Here, butter sold for seventeen cents a pound; wild ducks at forty to sixty cents a pair. "The butchers were artists in their own right," a local would recall. After the First World War, the building's gabled roof was flattened out when it was expanded for city offices. Yet a market remained, and the adjacent square was a gathering place, including for trade unionists during the 1919 strike. It was demolished to make room for the Public Safety Building and is planned to house a market once again.
**151 Princess Street.**

---

**CN Railways Office** 1942-1980s. Designed by John Schofield.

A state-of-the-art bunker on Portage, made to carry on essential telegraph and transport services in wartime. ("War needs come first," CN stated in a newspaper ad announcing the new building.) CN chief architect Schofield adopted suitably modern technologies—the four-storey structure was made of fireproof reinforced concrete—and modern style: its spare stone facade and strip windows hinted at European modernism.
**Now the 201 Portage office tower.**

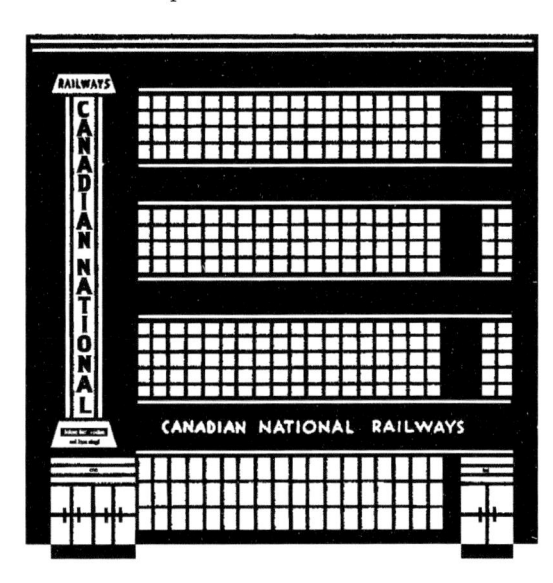

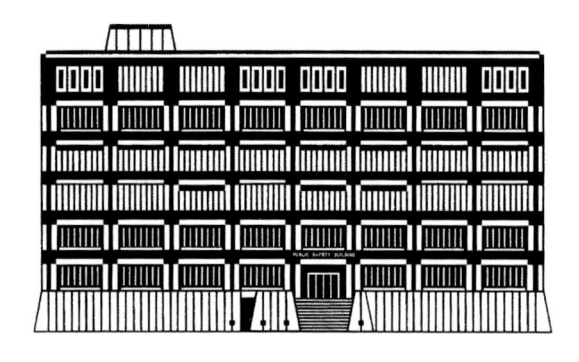

## Public Safety Building 1965-2020
Designed by Libling Michener & Associates.

Architecture that was brutalist and beautiful. This headquarters for the Winnipeg Police went up on the site of the Market Building. The local architects, led by young project architect Les Stechesen, employed the brutalist style then popular for civic buildings across the country, but rather than the expected concrete they chose hunks of Tyndall stone, rhyming with Winnipeg history and the material of the new city hall across the street. The building housed police offices, including the staff of the new 999 emergency line, as well as courtrooms and a jail. This sometimes dark history helped stall preservation efforts when the stone slabs began to come off. **151-171 Princess Street; now site of the Market Lands centre.**

---

## McArthur Building 1910-1988
Designed by John Russell.

The tallest building in the city, this would become the tallest ever demolished in Winnipeg. Lumber merchant and railroad magnate John McArthur saw the value of Portage Avenue frontage as the city grew. His wealth burgeoning, he hired architect Russell to create a $400,000 skyscraper, its top two floors supported by showy pediments. While the structure was steel, Russell took a conservative approach and kept the windows small and the walls sturdy with masonry. (Both McArthur and Russell kept offices here.) The Childs restaurant chain renamed the whole building in 1947, and it lasted through the 1980s, supplanted by the new tallest building in Winnipeg.
**211 Portage Avenue; now TD Centre.**

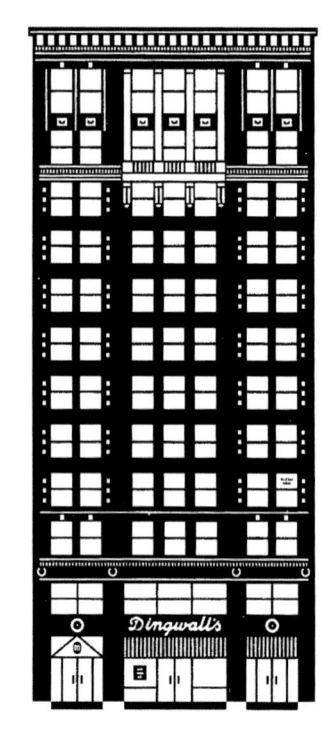

**Manitoba**

## Canadian Bank of Commerce 1899-1910
Designed by Darling & Pearson.

The Canadian Bank of Commerce came to Winnipeg in 1893 and soon constructed this temple of finance to serve the grain trade. The neo-classical building proved too small by 1910, and so the bank dismantled it to make room for a replacement, which still stands. The old structure was dismantled, reassembled in Regina in 1912, dismantled again in the 1970s, and partially reassembled again in the 1990s as four columns and a pediment in the atrium of that city's Cornwall Centre mall. **389 Main Street; now Millennium Centre.**

## McIntyre Block 1898-1979
Designed by Charles A. Barber and extended by James Cadham.

One of the city's great commercial addresses, McIntyre Block was a five-storey loft full of shops and offices. By the 1930s its Richardsonian Romanesque style was dated, and by 1977 it had lots of character but also many vacancies. At that point, the city was debating the merits of heritage preservation, and the McIntyre was at the centre. Developers and businessmen worried how the city would be perceived for having such old buildings at a prominent intersection. Today, there is a hole in the streetscape.
**416 Main Street; now a parking lot.**

**Manitoba**

**Royal Alexandra Hotel** 1906-1971
Designed by Edward and W.S. Maxwell.

The Canadian Pacific's local hotel was an opulent showpiece of railway-driven prosperity, and CP referred to it as an "expression of the nation's character." The railway tore down the shops of Jewish migrants to build it, and next door in the rail station new migrants arrived to be welcomed—or not. This seven-storey mass of stone and red brick would remain the biggest and poshest thing in the neighbourhood until the 1950s, when Queen Elizabeth stayed here; eight years later, it closed down. After its demolition, two Tyndall-stone lion heads from its facade wound up on display at a park off John Hirsch Place in the Exchange District. Today the Royal Alex site is still empty, but the attached train station is now the Neeginan Centre.
**183 Higgins Avenue.**

**Winnipeg International Airport Terminal** 1964-2012
Designed by Green, Blankstein & Russell.

A serious work of architecture for the jet age, this terminal stood among three contemporaries as first-rate modernist airports of Canadian design. Local architects GBR created a rigorously rectilinear building in the International Style, clad in local Tyndall stone. The gallery-like interior featured high-design Canadian furniture and commissioned works of art, including the large-scale pair of Eli Bornstein's *Structuralist Relief in Fifteen Parts* and John Graham's *Northern Lights*. A newspaper writer called it "the most exciting building in town." The increasing gigantism of the airport, however, left little room for preservation. Bornstein's piece was relocated to the University of Manitoba. **Now part of a new terminal.**

## REGINA, Saskatchewan

The city was built at a place roughly known in Cree as oskana kā-asastēki or Pile of Bones. (Its location was not an obvious place to settle, except that the colonial official in charge owned real estate nearby.) It was named to honour Queen Victoria, and after Saskatchewan's creation in 1905, it became the capital. Then it began to grow rapidly—from about three thousand to thirty thousand in a decade—as the province became the third largest in Canada. Not surprisingly, its architecture is rich with historicist styles that came with the first generations of settlers. Postwar growth and a long economic stall took their toll on the oldest parts of the city, as did the car. Parts of the city's built heritage are gone forever—for worse and for better.

---

**Travellers Building** 1929-2017. Designed by Storey & Van Egmond.

At first, this was a car dealership with the Arcadia Ballroom and Dance Studio upstairs. (The Arcadia had a horsehair dance floor.) Its owner, George Broder, developed his farm as Broder's Annex; once you bought a house there, a car would come in handy. It would also be useful for travelling salesmen, some of whom used office and display space upstairs. Later, this building became a bus depot and then it came to a stop, empty for two decades before it was torn down. **1833-43 Broad Street.**

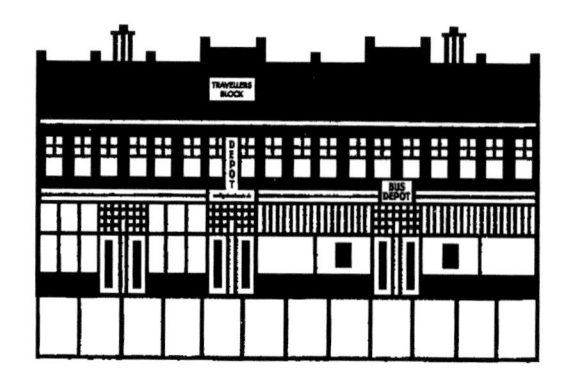

**City Hall** 1908-1965. William M. Dodd & E.C. Hopkins.

Regina's second city hall was known (like some other busy late-Victorian counterparts) as the Gingerbread Palace. Regina had become a city in 1903; in 1905, Saskatchewan became a province and chose Regina as its capital. The city grew to 30,213 people by 1911. This new Romanesque city hall was the seat of government and also a banquet hall, hosting fancy-dress balls and, reportedly, a boxing match. In 1968 a mall was built on the site, and it evolved into a federal public building again. (The cornerstone of this old city hall today sits on the southeast lawn of the current one.) **11th Avenue between Hamilton and Rose Streets; now the Alvin Hamilton Building.**

**Saskatchewan**

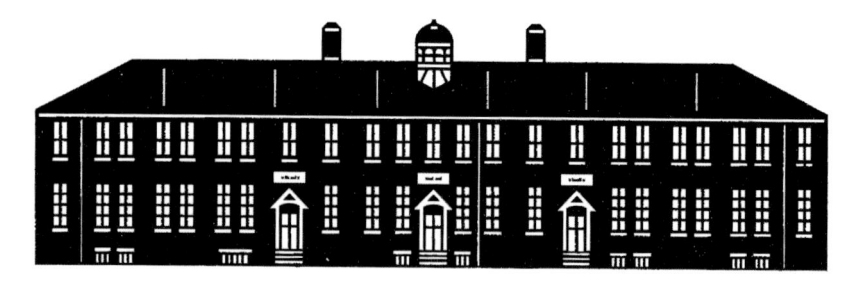

## Regina Indian Industrial School
1891-1948. Designed by Walter Chesterton.

From 1891 to 1910, children from First Nations and Métis communities in Saskatchewan, Alberta, and Manitoba were brought here. The Presbyterian Church and the federal government had straightforward goals: to Christianize them, assimilate them, and teach them a trade. "All influences should be used to break up the reservation and tribal systems," wrote the first principal, A.J. McLeod. One historian estimates one hundred children died here. At least thirty-five were buried in a cemetery on the site; their identities are mostly unknown. The school closed in 1910, becoming a jail and later a home for delinquent boys. It burned in 1948, and the only trace remaining is the cemetery. Its architect, Chesterton, joined the Royal Canadian Academy of Arts. **701 Pinkie Road, Pense.**

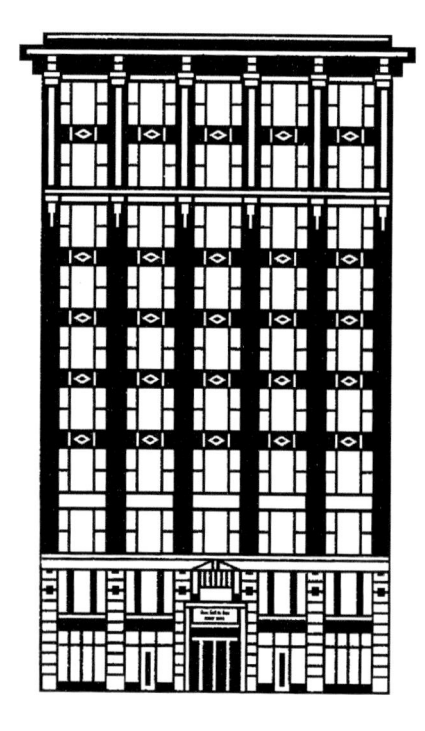

---

## McCallum Hill Building
1912-1982
Designed by Storey & Van Egmond.

At ten storeys, this was Regina's first skyscraper. Storey & Van Egmond, who built public buildings across Saskatchewan, delivered good Chicago Style architecture here: steel structure, applied stone facade, and a clear base, middle, and top. It took two hundred pounds of explosive to bring it down in 1982. Part of its facade was incorporated into its replacement, but that too was removed in the 1990s.
**Scarth Street and 12th Avenue; now Tower One of Hill Centre.**

## SASKATOON, Saskatchewan

The first settlers in Saskatoon were bent on self-denial. A group of Ontarians from the Temperance Colonization Society selected the site for a town, Nutana, in 1883. In 1890, the Qu'Appelle, Long Lake, and Saskatchewan Railway Company arrived here. Its station prompted growth on the west side of the river, where the liquor flowed freely while Nutana remained dry. The unified town incorporated in 1906, now with 4,500 people and the name of Saskatoon, after the Cree word for the abundant local berry. In the next decade, the optimistic city built Chicago Style loft buildings and castle-like high schools—stopped suddenly by the economic crash of 1913. In the next decades the city would grow, diversify, and sprawl. Many of the buildings of its first decades were wrecked as the fashion of urban renewal took hold, even here.

**Crowe Block** 1910-1984

A rare example of row houses in Saskatoon, Crowe Block was capped by a corbelled brick cornice and bookended by a restaurant that became the Corner Coffee Bar. A twin block to this one still stands across the street. The block had been recommended to council for heritage preservation before it was pulled down. **310-314 25th Street East; now a strip mall.**

## Queen's Hotel 1912-1980
Designed by Frank P. Martin.

The original Queen's Hotel was one of the first hotels in Saskatoon, built in 1892, just after the railway arrived. This larger five-storey replacement was a Beaux-Arts brick building with terracotta trim and pediments. By 1980, the Queen's was catering to long-term residents. On May 31, a major fire broke out, probably in the sauna. Forty-six firefighters came to battle it; two of them, Victor Budz and Dennis Guenter, perished. In the wake of the fire, the Saskatoon Fire Department changed its breathing equipment and increased its inspections of saunas. **1st Avenue South at 20th Street; now a parking garage.**

## Central Chambers 1911-1998
Designed by Thompson, Daniel & Colthurst.

Central Chambers was a workhorse of a downtown building and a fine example of what city planners call mixed use. Over the years it housed apartments, offices, restaurants, a furrier, and from 1924 to 1927, the Hotel Central. In 1927 and 1928, the city's public library found a temporary home in the building. A local developer bought the aging structure in the 1990s and demolished it for a single-storey retail strip. **219 22nd Street East; now stores.**

## Standard Trusts Building
1913-1976. Designed by William Fingland.

This six-storey tower went up during a major real estate boom before the First World War. The Winnipeg-based Fingland delivered a forward-looking architecture inspired by the Chicago School, its base and capital wrapped in expanses of terracotta. It was expected to be surrounded by even taller buildings, which never came. But the Saskatoon Art Centre started here in 1944; that artist-run centre would eventually became the Mendel Art Gallery. The Standard Trusts Building was eventually replaced by the Sturdy Stone Centre, after a huge controversy that helped birth the Saskatoon Heritage Society.
**102 3rd Avenue North; now Sturdy Stone Centre.**

---

## Parrish & Heimbecker Mill
1906-2015

Wheat helped build the city. Archie McNab built this mill for the Saskatoon Milling Company to process it — on his way to a career in business and politics, including as lieutenant-governor of Saskatchewan. Quaker Oats bought the Saskatoon Milling Company and ran it for most of a century, for many years as the Parrish & Heimbecker Company.
**Avenue N South at 18th Street.**

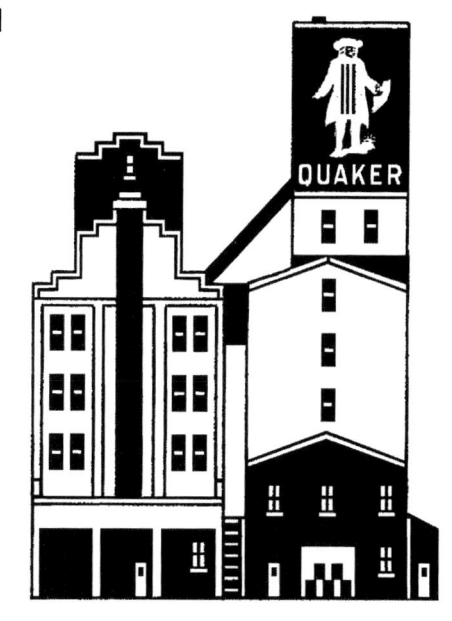

**Saskatchewan**

## Commodore Restaurant 1947-2007

Steve Leakos left the Greek mainland as a boy of fourteen and wound up in Saskatoon; here he was one of a half-dozen countrymen to run restaurants in the downtown. This one Leakos called the New Commodore to distinguish it from its predecessor on 21st Street. It was a hangout for the cooler high school kids, including, apparently, a young Joni Mitchell. The restaurant's name also appeared on sports jerseys: in the 1950s owner Spero Leakos was general manager of the semi-pro Saskatoon Commodores baseball team. The building became a Chinese restaurant, Chau's Commodore, and was demolished after a fire in 2007.

**108 2nd Avenue North; now a parking lot.**

## Board of Trade Building 1909-1938
Designed by Herbert J. Payton.

The birth of the Board of Trade reflected the success of the city: Saskatoon's population nearly tripled between 1909 and 1912. Located right in the path of arriving CN passengers, the board's building was all boomtown bluster: it had very tall floors (but only two of them), six Palladian windows (very close together), and a very small interior.

**1st Avenue South between 20th and 21st Streets; now Midtown Plaza.**

## CN Railway Station
1938-1966
Designed by John Schofield.

Saskatoon was known as Hub City for its place in the rail network that crossed the Prairies. By 1908, three railways were here, including CN. This stripped-classical station by CN's Schofield replaced an older station on the site, and it fell quiet when CN moved out of downtown in 1963. Midtown Plaza replaced this station and most of the yards behind it; meanwhile its predecessor, the 1908 CPR station, was saved from demolition in 1970 and is a recognized heritage building.
**1st Avenue and 22nd Street; now Midtown Plaza.**

---

## Early Seed & Feed 1914-1985

The Early family's hay, grain, and seed business became a staple in Saskatoon starting in 1907. (This was an era when every major city in the country had seed businesses in prominent locations.) In 1914 the Earlys built their new complex downtown, including a grain elevator painted with a large sign that advertised the business. Early's Farm and Garden Centre moved to a new location in the 1980s and is still operating today. **198 Idylwyld Drive South; now a Cactus Club Café.**

**Saskatchewan**

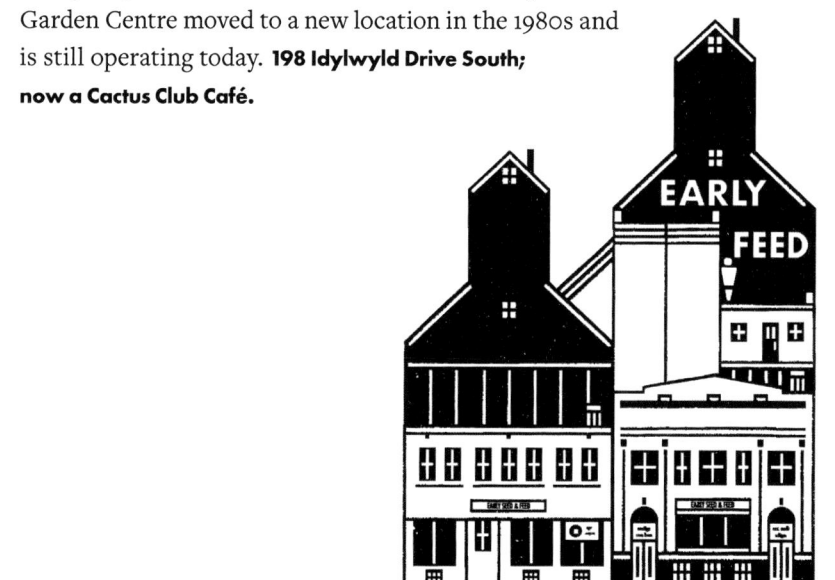

**Farnam Block** 1912-2015
Designed by Bugenhagen & Turnbull.

Here was a boom-time build that you would think had good bones. Its main architect, George Bugenhagen, was a trained bridge designer and structural engineer. A century later it housed Lydia's Pub, a beloved bar and music venue, and its owners thought it was unsalvageable. The brewery that replaced it uses some of the old building's wooden beams.
**650 Broadway Avenue; now Prairie Sun Brewery.**

---

**Capitol Theatre** 1929-1979. Designed by Murray Brown.

Famous Players delivered a spectacle on Second Avenue: the theatre's interior was decorated by the Maltese-Montréaler artist Emmanuel Briffa to look like a Spanish town. Despite the decline of cinema going in the 1970s, the building was almost saved at the wire. Politicians hoped to make a deal with the owners, but demolition crews started working over a weekend. Locals had salvaged many pieces of the building as keepsakes. As of 2019, the marquee was still in storage in a city yard. **127 2nd Avenue South; now Scotia Centre.**

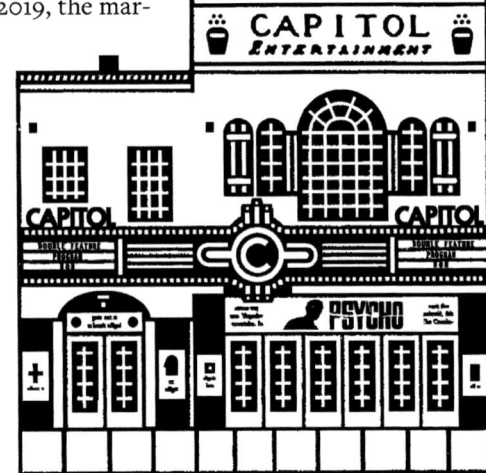

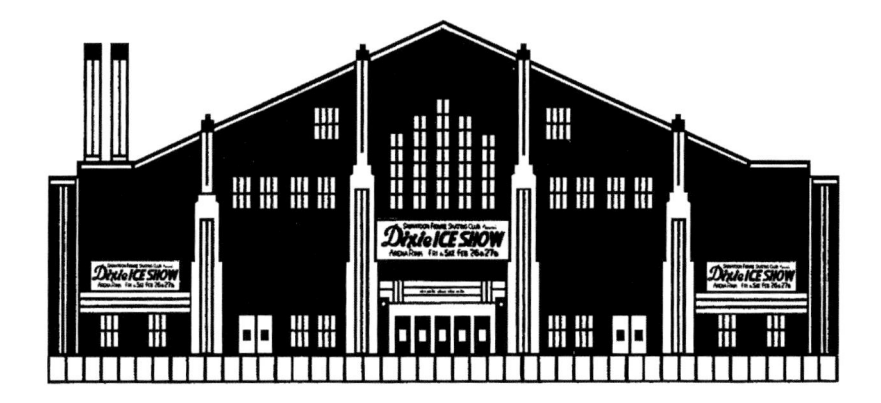

**19th Street Arena** 1937-1989. Likely designed by David Webster.

Known as the Barn, this was downtown's venue for skating, ice carnivals, the Saskatoon Quakers of the Western Hockey League, and for years, the Saskatoon Blades. Local politicians debated through the 1980s whether and how to replace it, winding up with SaskPlace. Meanwhile, it played host to Christian evangelists and Metallica. **Saunders Place; now the Remai Modern.**

---

**First Baptist Church** 1911-1943. Designed by Frank P. Martin.

For a corner site right next to the Crowe Block, Martin designed an asymmetrical and exuberant structure that translated neo-Gothic into the wooden language of the Prairies. A fire took this church in 1943, and a replacement remains on the site. (A pair of twin houses that Martin designed for himself and his brother still stands on Saskatchewan Crescent, extremely English and a bit out of place.) **25th Street East and 4th Avenue.**

**Saskatchewan**

## CNL Building 1917-1931

The Chinese Nationalist League, or Kuomintang, was China's ruling political party from 1927 to 1948. Many overseas Chinese were still very involved in politics, including men who came to Saskatoon in the late nineteenth century. The Chinese Exclusion Act of 1923 helped cement racist attitudes towards them and also prevented family reunification. In this context Chinese-owned businesses and communal organizations were crucial. However, the city demolished almost all of these, including the Kuomintang office, to build a new technical college. **129 19th Street East; now the Nutrien Tower site.**

---

## Saskatoon Main Public Library 1928-1965

The Saskatoon Public Library was established in 1913 as a reading room in the basement of an Oddfellows Hall. This, its first permanent home, was built in the neoclassical style of the Carnegie libraries but not actually funded by Andrew Carnegie, since locals refused a grant from the famous strikebreaker's "dirty money." By the 1960s the building was replaced by a new, much larger, modernist building that suited its larger role in the community. The chief librarian, Frances Morrison, was the first woman to occupy such a prominent position in Saskatoon, and the new library bears her name. **311 23rd Street East.**

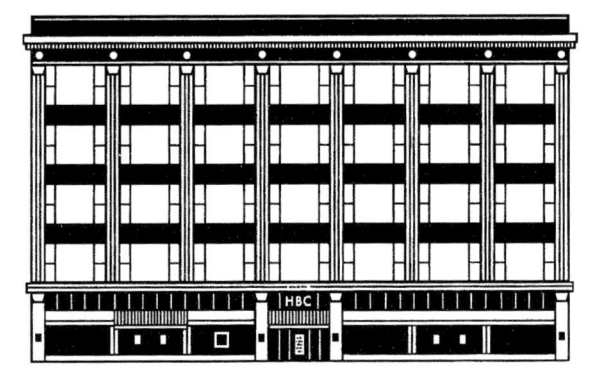

## Hudson's Bay Department Store
1913-1959
Designed by
G.H. Archibald and Co.

The J.F. Cairns Department Store commissioned this grand Chicago Style structure, made of fireproof steel and concrete, in 1913. Its business, and the building, were swallowed up by the Bay in 1922. (An internal Bay report that year noted that Saskatchewan "is the most populous of the three Prairie Provinces and from an agricultural standpoint the most developed and productive.") The Bay chartered all of the city's trams on opening day so that the city's twenty-five thousand people could ride to the store for free. In the 1950s the old structure was knocked down for a smaller replacement, which is still there, its decorative mosaics intact. **205 Second Avenue North; now a mixed-use building.**

---

### Royal Canadian Legion Building 1929-2007. Designed by David Webster.

Local First World War veterans built this, Branch No. 63 of the Royal Canadian Legion, and dedicated it to their dead comrades. (The architect, Webster, was himself wounded in battle. He would later become the province's deputy minister of public works.) The construction filled up the block where the city's Chinatown had just been levelled. By the 2010s the Legion was one of the oldest buildings in the south downtown; now it has been demolished as part of a new wave of redevelopment. **315 19th Street East; now the Nutrien Tower site.**

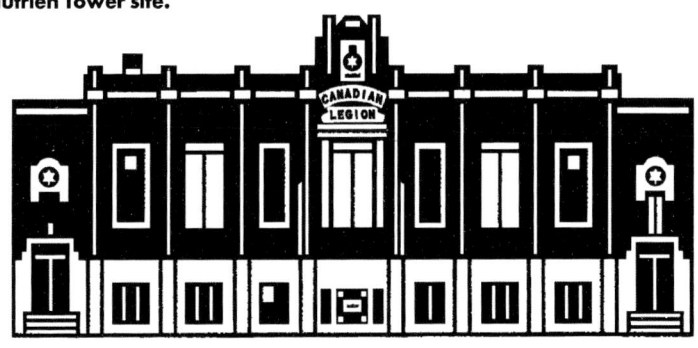

## Bank of Nova Scotia
1919-1979
Likely designed by Reginald E. McDonnell.

The Capitol Theatre with its marquee and Spanish tile roof delivered Spanish flair on Second Avenue; next door, this building (built for Merchant's Bank) offered a sober banker's counterpoint. Its rusticated stone base and broad cornice evoked a Florentine palazzo. The Bank of Nova Scotia occupied it for half a century before it was pulled down. **135 2nd Avenue South; now Scotia Centre.**

---

## Princess School 1911-1961. Designed by David Webster.

This and the neighbouring Alexandra School were the tallest and most impressive buildings of their day in Riversdale. The Princess stood three storeys tall with a round tower on top, its brick facades mixing Second Empire and a bit of Gothic. It was demolished in the 1960s, and its sister school was replaced in the 1980s. Now Princess Alexandra is poised to be the site of a combined new school, leaving other impressive buildings of the era with an uncertain future.

**720 20th Street at Avenue H; now a commercial building.**

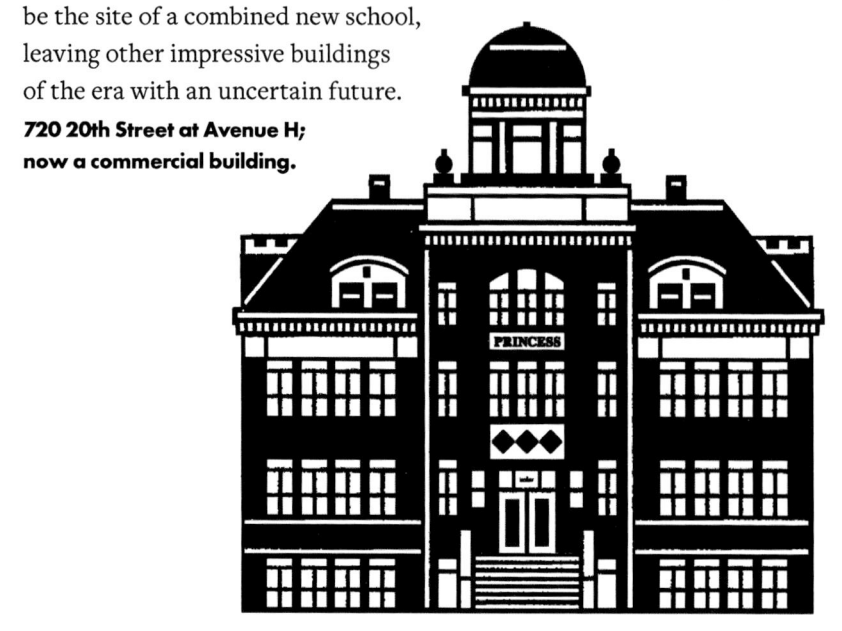

**Saskatchewan**

**Gatineau Club** 1909-1962

In the boom years around 1910, alcohol was still a fraught topic in Saskatoon. Temperance advocates and drinkers battled for political influence. While "ban-the-bar" legislation passed in 1915, it was possible to find a drink if you knew where to look, but not here: this hotel, then called the Temperance, was the only one in the area without a bar. New owners (remembered in the local newspaper as "some Chinese") renamed it Canada House and later the Gatineau Club. Its octagonal, turret-topped tower provided a rare flourish until the building was condemned in 1958 and burned three years later. Meanwhile, its founder led an interesting life: the London-born Alfred Bailey became a prospector, then served on the British merchant cruiser HMS *Rajputana* in the Second World War, aged fifty-five. He barely escaped when his ship was torpedoed in 1941.
**Avenue B and 24th Street West.**

---

**Fire Hall No. 1** 1908-1965. Designed by Walter LaChance.

The terracotta sign up top read FIRE HALL and so it was: a four-bayed white-brick structure topped by a Baroque tower and cupola. This was architecture for a growing city department embracing the twentieth century. (The first motorized fire truck would arrive three years later.) It was demolished, alongside the library next door, to make room for the new Frances Morrison Public Library.
**23rd Street and
4th Avenue.**

**Saskatchewan**

## CALGARY, Alberta

The Bow and Elbow Rivers move through here, but history moves more quickly. Or at least it has since the Canadian Pacific Railway rolled through in 1883, and where there had once been the Niitsitapi (Blackfoot), then a handful of settlers, suddenly there was a colonial town. A decade later, it was incorporated as a city; a generation later, it was a place worthy of the name. The wealth of trading, farming, and ranching gathered around the train station, and soon the one- and two-storey wooden buildings of downtown gave way to larger ones of brick and sandstone. (Fire taught Calgarians the value of a stone face.) Homesteading, gas, and—above all—oil left their mark on the city. So did the car, as Calgary scattered outward beginning in the 1940s, and much of the central city was reshaped and razed in the name of automotive convenience. What was lost along the way? Ranchers' mansions. Some of the places where old Calgary had gathered, such as the Capitol Theatre. Hotels that had put up the city's workers. Even a handsome stone office building, which stood in the way as the city shifted like a river.

### Art Central
1928-2013

At first it was a place for necessities: a solidly built grocery store on a bustling block of downtown. Then it had many lives, as old buildings do, until it was converted to Art Central—a complex of artists' studios and boutiques. The 2008 bust put an end to that: as its landlord said, art is not at the top of the list of things to buy during a recession. But the site's future is distinguished: it's now home to the Telus Sky tower, a new city landmark.
**619 Centre Street South.**

## Capitol Theatre

1921-1972

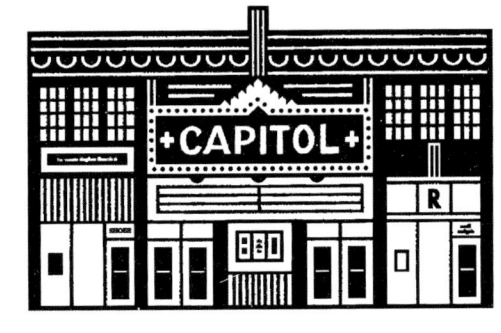

"A sizzling trip through the West and the land of romance!" That was the tagline for *The Love Special* with Wallace Reid, which played here on opening night in 1921. Out front, a shimmering marquee livened up the staid brick facade; you could buy shoes in one storefront, confectionary in the other. Inside the 1,560-seat space, a block-long room lit by crystal chandeliers, silents alternated with vaudeville performances until the Capitol brought Calgary its first talkies. It all came down in 1972, along with the neighbouring Royal Hotel, for what became Stephen Avenue Place—a place with less drama, less romance, fewer shimmering lights. **7th Avenue Southwest; now Calgary Courts Centre.**

---

## Summit Sheraton Hotel 1965-1989. Designed by William G. Milne.

A cylindrical hotel? In 1965, it made sense. "The economy of the practical circular structure," an advertisement claimed, "has permitted the Summit management to spend more money on interior finishings...to produce rich and satisfying results." The architecture's quirky modernist form blended with interior designer Arthur Fishman's "Spanish and Italian" details—including the Medici family crest. It was eventually topped off with an S for Sheraton and then later pulled down for a parking lot.
**202 4th Avenue Southwest.**

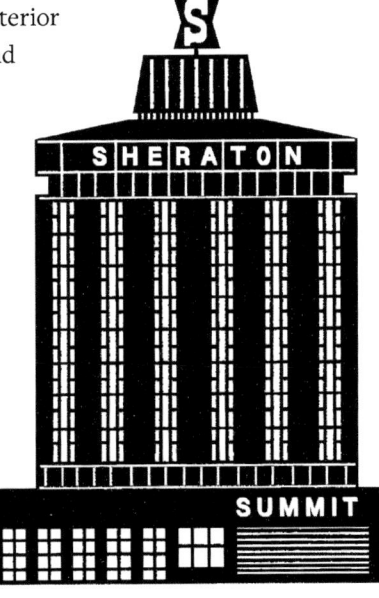

## Hotel York 1928-2007

Designed by Jacob Knoepfli with Merrill Owens.

This was always a place to live modestly, but it had some art deco flash. Owens, a film-set designer, created friezes in blue and red bas-relief, working with the novel material of cast-in-place concrete. These lush designs blended bits of botany with hints of Ancient Egypt. Still, the hotel advertised "reasonable rents." And after decades occupied by all sorts of workers and travellers, the city took it over for highly affordable housing in the 1990s. A decade later, it was torn down for the construction of the Bow Building complex next door. The decorative panels were disassembled and stored, ready to be attached to a new eight-storey building, but an economic bust ended that plan. Today the site remains a public plaza, and Owens's handiwork remains somewhere out of sight. **Centre Street and 6th Avenue Southeast; now the Bow Building plaza.**

---

## CPR Station 1911-1966. Designed by Walter Scott Painter.

The CP railway was Calgary's main artery, bringing people and prosperity, and this was its bright, stony heart. The grand two-storey arrival hall was where new Calgarians arrived and tourists passed through — perhaps to spend a night next door at the Palliser Hotel, which towered over downtown. The station's masonry front gave it the aspect of a temple, though a temple whose front was busy with carts and automobiles. Today the arches on Palliser Square nod to the station that stood here. **115 9th Avenue Southeast; now Palliser Square.**

## Telstar Drug
1962-2006

In 1962, all the world was talking about the American satellite that would bring the world to our living rooms, connecting Paris with London and New York with Calgary. And all that ambition and global glitz landed on the roof of a drugstore at 14th and Kensington—giant sans-serifs announcing the space age. The Bergh family's establishment would last four decades, and the sign now resides at the Glenbow Museum. The actual Telstar, meanwhile, went dark after a year. **1413 Kensington Road Northwest; now shops.**

---

## Fire Hall No. 1 1887-1911

Sometimes the face of a city changes in a flash. For Calgary this came in 1886, when a fire swept through downtown and consumed most of its wooden structures. The city's buildings soon came back with faces of brick and stone, but they still had wooden bones—which meant this institution was badly needed. This structure rose high above the streetscape, its church-like form capped with a chunky tower that cradled a 1,500-pound bell. Down below, three bays held horses and carts, who protected the city for a generation. **7th Avenue Southeast; now a Royal Canadian Legion hall.**

## Cecil Hotel 1912-2015

The Cecil Hotel came in with a boom, and went out with a flood. The "workingman's hotel" with bar and barbershop opened in 1912 to serve railroad workers and mechanics. The founders were German immigrants, printers Charles Pohl and Joseph Schuster, who ran a newspaper called *Der Deutsche Canadier* out back of the hotel. The First World War ended the paper and Pohl's time in Canada, but the hotel survived as a steady presence in the East Village; the neon sign on the roof shouted its name for half a century. The bar became a gathering place for Calgary's queer women, and then a rougher crowd, attracting lots of police attention, and after a murder, it closed down in 2008. The floods of 2013 hit the place hard, bringing rain and decay inside its gabled roof, and two years later it came down. **401 4th Avenue Southeast; now a parking lot.**

---

## Hull House 1905-1970

Hull House was a grand manse built by beef. Rancher and meatpacker William Roper Hull helped shape Calgary's high society and its buildings, funding its opera house and grain exchange. His wealth remained vast: when he died in 1925, his estate was valued at $1,653,353. He built himself a grand house in the Bow Valley, which survives, and this city house. Square in plan, it had an ornately neoclassical front porch, a tile roof, and stone quoining set into the brick. The Glenbow Foundation bought the house in 1955, and it was their headquarters until it was demolished fifteen years later.
**12th Avenue and 5th Street Southwest.**

## Hull's Opera House 1893-1963
Designed by Child & Wilson.

This structure began as a place of culture. Not opera, on its first night, but a schoolchildren's music festival; the *Calgary Herald* reported that "the hall was well lighted and the temperature was about right." Perhaps Calgary was not yet Milan. This long, barnlike hall, whose front facade was decorated with sandstone accents, Romanesque arches, and stained glass, housed cultural events until 1906, when it was converted into shops with apartments above. Then, in the sixties, it became a parking lot.
**606 Centre Street South; now Hanover Place.**

## CPR Department of Natural Resources 1911-1966

At first the station had a public garden next door. But CP soon found itself in other lines of business, including coal, oil, and gas in Alberta and British Columbia. The garden disappeared, filled in by this stone-faced five-and-a-half-storey pile that stood taller than the station itself. Its neoclassical pomp, capped with a balustrade, gave way to something distinct, modern, and much taller: the Calgary Tower. **9th Avenue Southeast; now the Calgary Tower.**

## Robin Hood Flour Mills
1910-1973
Mill building designed by R.G. Gordon.

A towering symbol of the Prairies' natural wealth, this set of concrete structures began with a mill for the Calgary Milling Company. Later it belonged to the International Milling Company, and two grain elevators towered over 9th Avenue, nearly windowless and enormous. (The modern architect Le Corbusier loved the purposeful brawn of grain elevators and called them "the magnificent first fruits of the new age.") Indeed, this complex was a massive machine, with storage for over a million bushels of wheat that was milled into Robin Hood–brand flour. The giant Robin Hood logos overlooked the city from two sides well into the 1960s, when the mill closed and, soon after, was torn down for an office tower. **401 9th Avenue Southwest; now Gulf Canada Square.**

---

## Moravian Church 1902-c. 1970

A committed Protestant sect came from Russia seeking religious freedom and found it in a little shingled wooden church with triangular-arched door and windows, three on each side, pointing upward toward the divine. Today, something very worldly and horizontal has replaced the building: a parking garage.
**7th Avenue and 3rd Street Southeast.**

## Westbourne Baptist Church c. 1910-2017

This is where Bill Aberhart's *Back to the Bible Hour* radio show began. Before Aberhart founded the Social Credit party and began his rise in politics—he was Alberta's premier from 1935 to 1943—he preached over the radio from this, his home church in the now-vanished neighbourhood of Victoria Park. The red-brick structure was well built and without much ornament, as "Bible Bill" surely would have wanted. **Olympic Way Southeast and 13th Street Southeast; now a parking lot next to Cowboys Casino.**

## Land Titles Office 1907-1970. Designed by Allan M. Jeffers.

When pieces of Calgary were bought and sold, the details were recorded here, often by hand. And the place was appropriately ceremonial. At the top of the front steps, two columns supported a heavy portico, above which hung the provincial coat of arms. This was a place where weighty information would rest safely: the guts were concrete and brick, the facades all sandstone, none of it flammable. When the office came down in 1970, pieces of the stone were salvaged to patch up other structures. **601 5th Street Southwest; now the Alberta Court of Queen's Bench.**

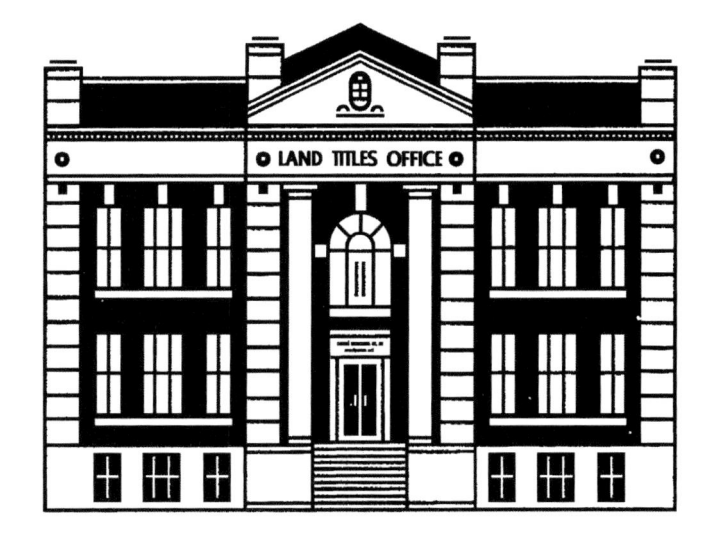

**Burns Manor** 1901-1956. Designed by Francis Rattenbury.

This was the home of a giant in Western Canada: Pat Burns, the rancher and meatpacker who was one of the four founders of the Calgary Stampede. Burns's country house, which anchored vast land holdings, is now the Bow Valley Ranche Restaurant in Fish Creek Provincial Park. For this, his city house, he called the architect Francis Rattenbury, who famously designed the BC Legislature. The grand centre-hall manse had Gothic ornament carved into its sandstone front—and a three-storey stone tower stuck to one side, like some fragment of an Irish castle that had lost its way. This slightly unwieldy place (like many mansions of the era) became an institution, serving as a hospital during the Second World War. When it was demolished in the 1950s, Calgarians flocked in to buy up doors, fixtures, and hunks of stone, some of which were used to create a rock garden named for Burns. **501 13th Avenue Southwest; now the Sheldon Chumir Health Centre.**

## Alexander Corner 1890-1920
Designed by Child and Wilson.

Calgary's first architecture office, Child and Wilson (who also created the Alberta Hotel), designed this building of shops and offices with flair. The rough-cut stone formed Romanesque arches at the sidewalk, rising up to two intersecting gables, with a turret at the corner. It's perhaps because of that gesture that the building became known as Alexander Corner. Its upper floors were home to mining and oil companies and later the Retail Clerks' Assocation—until retail, in the form of the Hudson's Bay Company, wiped the place out for an expansion of its store. **8th Avenue and 1st Street Southwest; now part of The Bay.**

## St. George's Island Bandstand 1911-1949

In 1887, the frontier town of Calgary took over three islands in the Bow River as parks, naming them after the patron saints of the United Kingdom: St. Patrick, St. Andrew, and St. George. The latter became an important gathering place, and in 1912 the city built this two-storey structure as a biergarten, at a cost of $4,560. But beer was soon illegal, and the downstairs became a teahouse. The structure's delicate gingerbread trim suited this new use—though boisterous music from upstairs often disrupted tea. **Now part of the Calgary Zoo grounds.**

**Alberta**

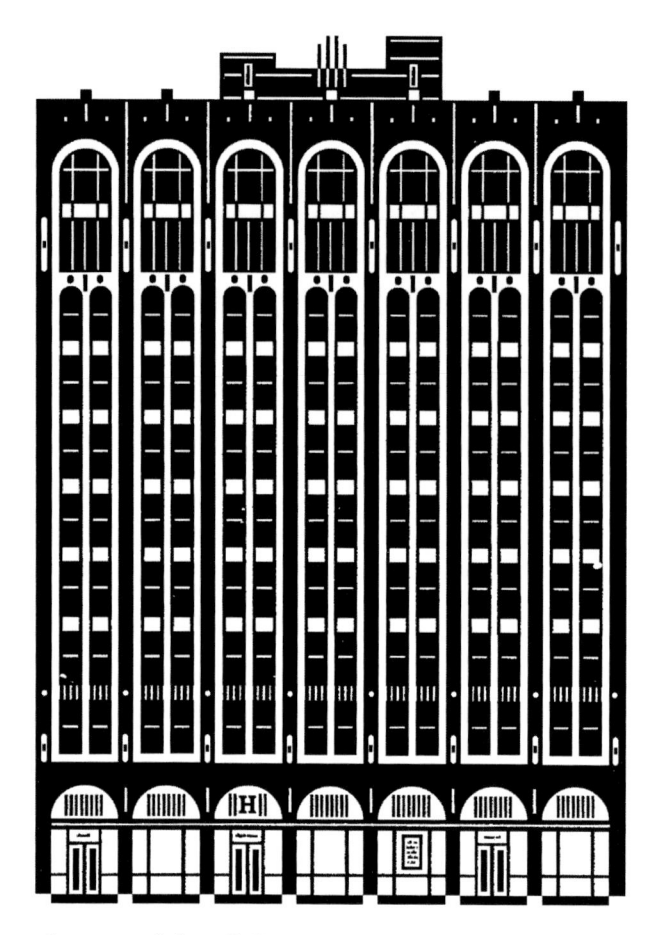

**The Herald Building** 1913-1972. Designed by Brown & Vallance.

The *Herald* was a central institution in the city, and this ten-storey tower designed in the Gothic Revival style by Montréal architects and faced with a mix of brick, sandstone, and terracotta was fit for a king, or at least an editor. From the second floor, a line of gargoyles looked down at the street: the two architects and a series of newsroom characters from the editor down to a printer's devil (assistant apprentice). The building went down in 1972 after serving as a Greyhound bus terminal. Copies of the gargoyles were added to the Alberta Hotel in the 1970s, and some original figures survived. These days they live in the Calgary Telus Convention Centre.
**130 7th Avenue Southwest; now the Len Werry Building.**

## EDMONTON, Alberta

Fur traders travelled the North Saskatchewan River, encountering several Indigenous groups including Cree, Saulteaux, and Niitsitapi, but its deep valley here made Edmonton less of a river port than its Prairie counterparts. Instead it grew up on the flats, initially to the north, where the Hudson's Bay Company survey defined an urban area that the city soon overspilled, and the Calgary and Edmonton Railway's development of Strathcona stretched the city to one side. Large-scale building didn't really begin until after 1900, when the city drew on the Beaux-Arts style and on influences (and architects) from Montréal and the United States. The postwar period brought additions, including some fine Modern architecture, but also considerable losses as the city abandoned and demolished some landmarks of the previous generations.

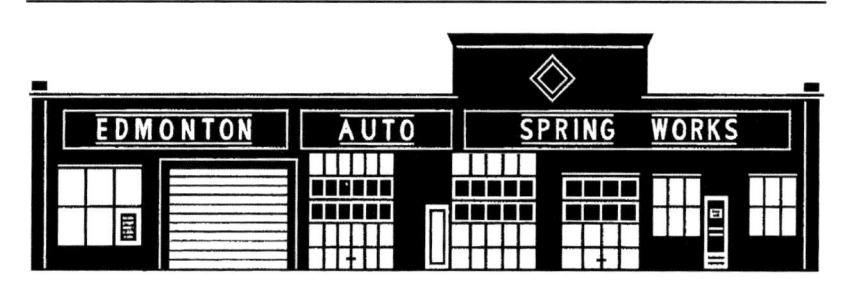

### Edmonton Auto Spring Works 1924-2010

In the 1920s, cars began to take over the city, and auto garages displaced stables and liveries. This sleek stucco-clad garage brought a fittingly modern architectural language, and its loud signage would become a landmark for half a century until a fire brought the place down. **9502 102nd Avenue Northwest.**

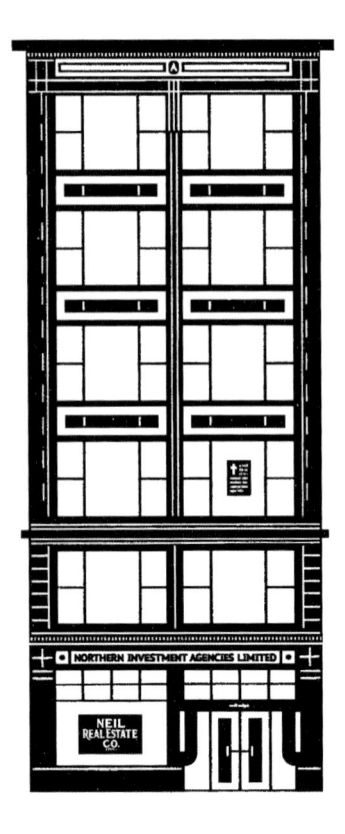

**The Agency Building** 1912-1972
Designed by MacDonald & Magoon.

Twenty-five feet wide and six storeys tall, this long, narrow tower made the most of expensive land. It also adopted from booming Chicago the latest in reinforced-concrete structure and broad windows. In later years its height made it a prime spot for neon signs on Jasper Avenue, first for Northwestern Utilities Natural Gas and later for Shell, always accompanied by painted signs for the building itself. The single-stair building became less desireable in time, but land remained expensive, and it made way for a much larger office complex.
**10057 Jasper Avenue; now the First and Jasper Building.**

---

**The Gem Theatre** 1913-2010. Designed by MacDonald & Magoon.

Leonard Goodridge (who also built the nearby Goodridge Building) constructed this theatre in the Edwardian classical style. Some moderne details were added in the 1930s, and a flashy marquee kept advertising films until 1957. Then the two-storey building served many purposes, including a Chinese cultural centre and a nightclub called the Gem Ballroom. In 1979, it changed back into a movie theatre showing Chinese-language films. This was the moment when the city's old Chinatown was being razed for the new Canada Place complex. By the 2000s the theatre was closed and rundown. Preservation and development plans went nowhere, and the city demolished the crumbling structure for safety. **9682 Jasper Avenue.**

**Imperial Bank** 1907-1950
Designed by Johnson & Barnes.

For the Imperial Bank's third location, local architect J. Percy Barnes designed a temple of capital. The three-and-a-half-storey structure on what was then the corner of Jasper and McDougall Streets featured a portico with heavy Tyndall stone columns. The interior boasted Alberta sandstone, bronze grilles, and Spanish marble—quality materials sending a message of wealth and security. By the 1940s it was torn down (no easy thing) to make way for a bigger building, just as the Imperial Bank would become part of a bigger bank.
**9990 Jasper Avenue; now the World Trade Centre.**

**Edmonton Public Library** 1923-1968. Designed by MacDonald & Magoon.

The sign above the door read FREE TO ALL, and this library, funded by the industrialist Andrew Carnegie, provided free access to books in grand Beaux-Arts surroundings. "Here rests the wisdom-treasure of mankind," read a poem in the opening day's program. This treasure was late in coming. Edmonton had seventy thousand people by then, and Calgary, already a rival, had opened its own Carnegie library a decade earlier. But the new building represented all sorts of change; one of its designers was Esther Marjorie Hill, who was the first woman in Canada to graduate from an architecture program. The Sixties brought a new library, and, in this city of boom and bust, nobody much complained when the Carnegie building was wrecked. **10020 100th Street; now ATB Place.**

## McDougall Mansion 1900-1974
Designed by William S. Edmiston & Henry D. Johnson.

John McDougall started out as a teacher and wound up as Edmonton's fourth mayor and a successful businessman. His lines included furs, outfitting, and trading exploitatively in the land certificates issued to Métis people. All this paid off well and funded this two-and-a-half-storey late-Victorian mansion. Like many urban mansions in the decades after the Second World War, it was used by children's and health care institutions, including the YMCA, which tore it down.
**9936 103rd Street; now Claire Estates.**

---

## Corona Hotel 1932-1983. Designed by MacDonald & Magoon.

The first Corona Hotel was built by one of Edmonton's first architects, James Edward Wize, who ran the hotel until his death. A 1932 gas fire destroyed that building—and led to serious litigation and a new policy in Edmonton to add an odour to natural gas. The replacement hotel saw the dominant local architects employ some Tudor-meets-art deco ornamentation. Its name survives in that of the transit station on the site.

**10665 Jasper Avenue; now the Corona LRT Station.**

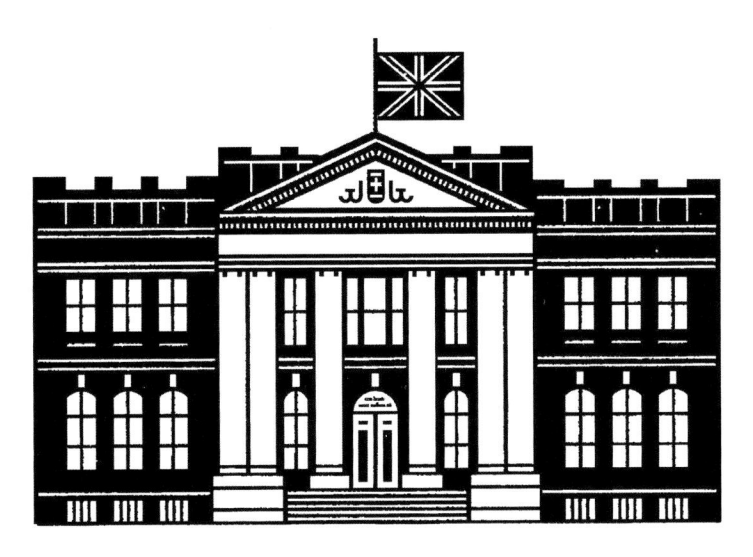

**Edmonton Court House** 1912-1972. Designed by Allan Merrick Jeffers.

In its early years of settlement Edmonton had various makeshift courthouses, including the upstairs of a saloon. This was the first purpose-built courthouse; provincial architect Jeffers had recently designed the legislature building (and the state capitol in Rhode Island, which the legislature closely resembles). Here, he used Alberta sandstone for not one but two grand entrances, one facing each side, with the provincial seal carved above. (It "left nothing wanting from an architectural standpoint," his office said in a statement.) The courthouse was extended with a modernist addition in 1955, but even that soon proved too small. Woolworth's tore the building down for a new store. **10221 100th Street; now City Centre.**

---

**M&R Auction House** 1908-2016

This was not one building but actually four, collected behind a three-storey "boomtown front" that lent an air of grandeur. It spent its last thirty years as a cultural venue, first the Sunlight Cafe and then the Artery, a hub for music, the Fringe Festival, and the Poetry Festival. The Artery was closed suddenly and torn down in 2016 to provide a staging area for transit construction. Nothing has replaced it. **9535 Jasper Avenue.**

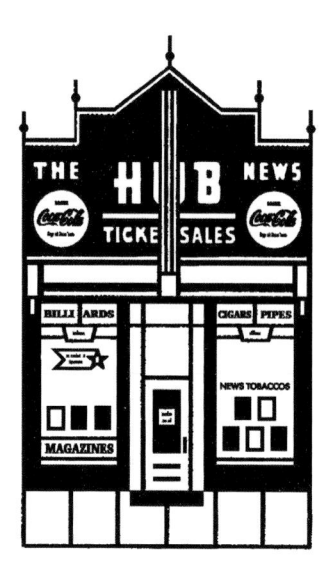

## Hub Cigar 1894-2005

The railway arrived in Strathcona in 1891. Three years later, J.J. Duggan spent $300 to construct this newsstand and serve travellers. The Hub outlasted him, the amalgamation of Strathcona with Edmonton, and much else. By the end, it was Western Canada's oldest newsstand. The reconstructed building bears the name of the Hub but not its signs or trade.

**10345 82nd Avenue; now a shop**

## CN Railway Station 1928-1966. Designed by John Schofield.

This was another railway showpiece, with concrete structure and faces of red brick and Tyndall stone. The station featured a skylit, double-height waiting room; interior finishes of terrazzo, oak, and fir; and a restrained Edwardian classical facade, oriented to be seen from Jasper Avenue. The station anchored a huge twenty-track rail yard, and passengers could still board from the basement of the CN Tower right up into the 1990s.

**10004 104th Avenue; now the CN Tower.**

## Sache House 1900-1962

Frederick Sache moved from Ontario in 1872 with a survey party and became an early resident and land speculator in Strathcona. He and his wife, Mary, raised three children here, intitially in a log cabin and then in a typical Prairie Vernacular farmhouse, with gabled roof, two chimneys, and a bay window. Strathcona grew to surround the house, and in 1962 Sache House was replaced by an apartment building.
**10048 88th Avenue.**

---

## Tegler Building 1911-1982. Designed by MacDonald & Magoon.

"Edmonton's skyscraper." That is how the *Edmonton Bulletin* referred to this, the city's tallest building of the era. Its brick-and-stone Edwardian classical walls housed a department store and more than one hundred offices, and even more after a 1912 expansion. The Bank of Montréal moved to tear it down in the late 1970s, and after a long debate proceeded to do so on live TV. The demolition helped seed the local heritage preservation movement, and now the bank that replaced it has itself been demolished.
**10189 101st Street.**

## The Duncan Block 1896-2003

This set of shops and apartments made it into the twenty-first century as a strip of independent businesses. An overnight fire took out most of the block, including the former drugstore at the corner that had become a family restaurant with Old-West-meets-Las Vegas signage. The replacement was a Starbucks. **10370 82nd Avenue.**

## Downtown Post Office 1910-1972. Designed by David Ewart.

The largest building in Edmonton when it was built, this reflected the work of the federal Department of Public Works in local Tyndall stone. It featured a rusticated stone base, topped by an entablature, itself capped by a steeply sloped mansard roof and then a forty-metre clock tower. After it closed in 1966, it was eventually demolished. The tower was dismantled and its stone used for a monument in the Evergreen Memorial Gardens. The clock itself remains on the site.
**10135 100th Street; now the Westin Hotel.**

**Varscona Theatre** 1940-1987. Designed by Rule, Wynn & Rule.

The local Suburban Theatres chain hired one of Alberta's leading twentieth-century architecture firms to outdo the competition, and this 1940 design delivered flash and swagger: a tall pylon protruded above a swooping marquee, whose composition balanced a curve on one end with a circular window on the other. Behind this fine Streamline Moderne composition were nearly five hundred seats, and the theatre prospered until the VCR era. It was replaced by a bank whose architecture echoed that of the theatre; the bank, in turn, was demolished for a Shoppers Drug Mart.
**10917 82nd Avenue.**

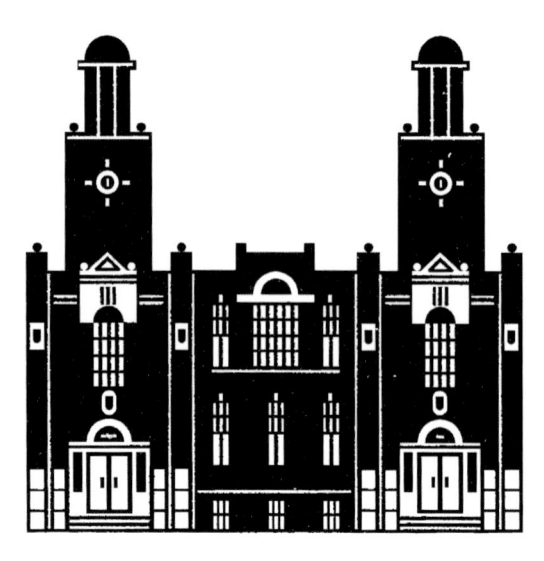

**Victoria School** 1911-1962. Designed by Roland Lines.

This was originally named Edmonton High School because it was going to be the only one in the city. Its architect—who would die in battle during the First World War—delivered a $150,000 structure that combined towers topped with finials, rusticated arches borrowed from a Florentine palazzo, and an underground gym. A new modernist building was constructed in 1949, with later additions. The "Old Vic" carried on to 1962.
**10842 102nd Street; now Victoria School of the Arts.**

---

**Edmonton Journal Building** 1921-1990. Designed by William Blakey.

Moving out of a downtown block that would house the Tegler Building, the newspaper found a new site for its newsroom, presses, and multimedia empire, adding a twenty-three-metre tall tower for radio broadcasts. (The presses sometimes drowned out the broadcasts.) Blakey designed a playfully asymmetric Edwardian classical building for them, which gave way in the eighties to something shinier. Fragments of the 1921 building remain on display inside the current one. **10006 101st Street.**

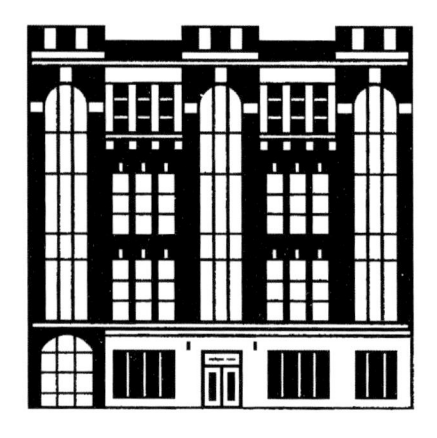

## Edmonton Art Gallery 1969-2007. Designed by Bittorf & Wensley Architects.

The gallery's first purpose-built structure was a creature of the times: a well-proportioned box of board-formed concrete with a concrete pavilion on top, brutalist from top to bottom. A design competition led to a near-total renovation by former Frank Gehry staffer Randall Stout. Also on the competition shortlist was Zaha Hadid, which suggests a fascinating architectural road not taken. **2 Sir Winston Churchill Square; now the Art Gallery of Alberta.**

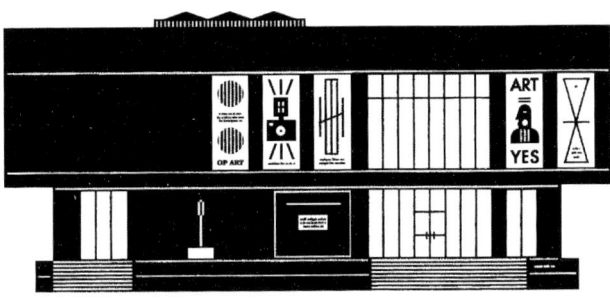

## Arlington Apartments 1909-2008. Designed by Barnes & Gibbs.

The city's first large-scale apartment block was built to attract a growing professional class, offering a marble entrance atrium, built-in oak furniture, and an upstairs tea room. Its layout, with a central corridor and apartments on both sides, became a template for similar buildings across the West. Like its peers, the building went downhill after the Second World War, when homeownership and the suburbs lessened its allure, but it was still occupied when an arsonist damaged it heavily in 2005. After that, it was seen as beyond saving. **10524 100th Avenue.**

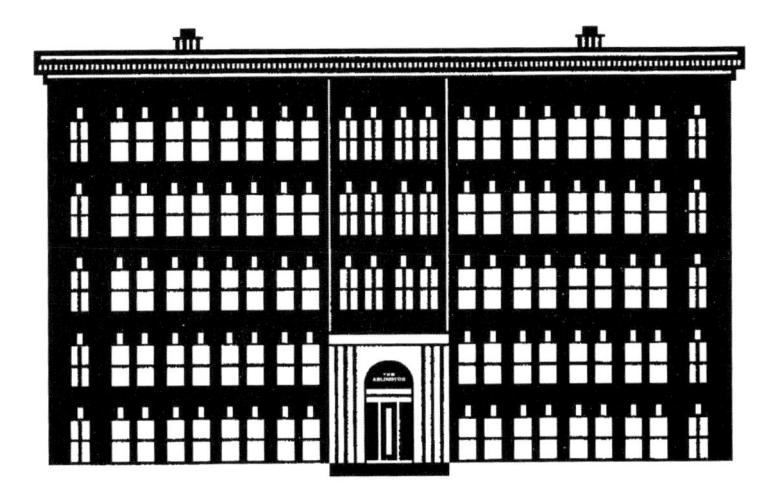

**Edmonton Gardens** 1913-1982

Originally built as the Edmonton Stock Pavilion, the city's first indoor arena was long known as the Cow Barn. Comfortable it wasn't; by the sixties it had old wooden seats, view-blocking girders, and a leaky roof. A renovation added a modernist front entrance and new bones, and it opened again in 1967 for a few more years of service, including the first seasons of the Oilers. The new concrete proved strong: demolition crews tried dynamiting it twice before resorting to a wrecking ball. **7515 118th Avenue; now Edmonton Expo Centre.**

# LETHBRIDGE, Alberta

Settlers began drift-mining coal in the river valley in the mid-nineteenth century, having displaced the Niitsitapi. In the 1880s the town was laid out and a brickyard opened. For decades, only brick was allowed in the central city; settlers understood the dangers of the dry, windy climate. The city boomed between 1907 and 1913, creating the High Level Bridge and a stock of buildings that wouldn't be matched for half a century. The city's growth slowed and sputtered, and then in the postwar era it sped up—losing things along the way, including a hub for Chinese railway workers and a grand hotel built on the wealth of wheat.

## Chinese National League Building 1910-2011

In 1913, the local branch of the Chinese National League, or Kuomintang, took over this building as its lodge hall. Because city bylaws restricted Chinese ownership of land, it was located across the street from its rival organization, known (through loose translation) as the Chinese Freemasons. The CNL was a political organization, but the building was also a place for newly arrived immigrants—usually men, without their families—to live and socialize, and a school in back provided Chinese-language education until the 1970s. Though the building's history was recognized with heritage protection, there was a lack of funding to repair and maintain it as a historic site.

**309 2nd Avenue South; now a parking lot.**

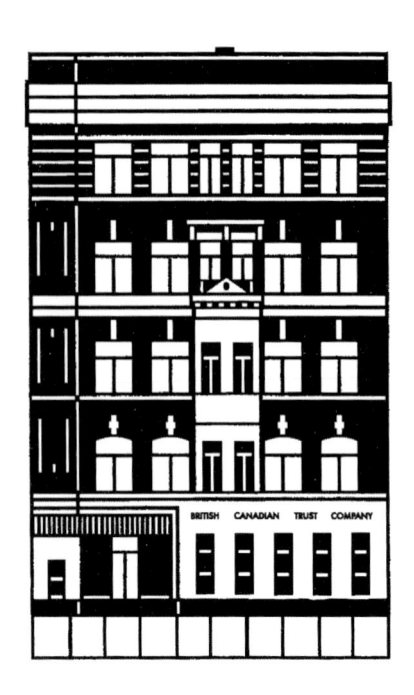

## Sherlock Block 1909-1982
Designed by Edward Ernest Carver.

This building was three storeys at the start and was soon extended to five, which made it the tallest building in Lethbridge. The architect Carver designed it with brick facades (Mr. Sherlock was in the brick business), but Carver's design showed off the building's state-of-the-art concrete structure in horizontal bands at the top. Carver set up shop here himself, between other offices and apartments; later this became the Canada Trust Building.
**306 7th Street South; now shops.**

## Capitol Theatre 1911-1974. Designed by William H. Meech.

Opened as a vaudeville house called the Morris in 1911, this theatre went through a series of names until 1929, when it experienced a major renovation and reopened as the Capitol. Meech, a British-trained architect who had recently been the city's commissioner of public works, delivered a swoopy moderne facade. Fittingly, the theatre was one of the first in the region to start showing talkies. **414 5th Street South; now Lethbridge Centre.**

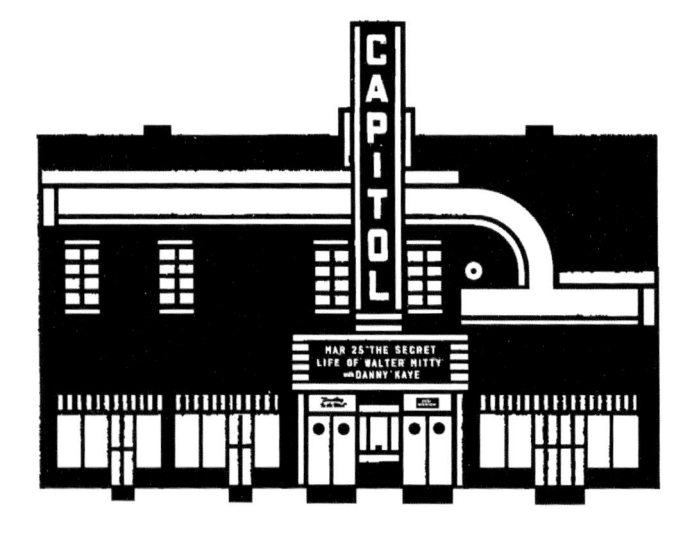

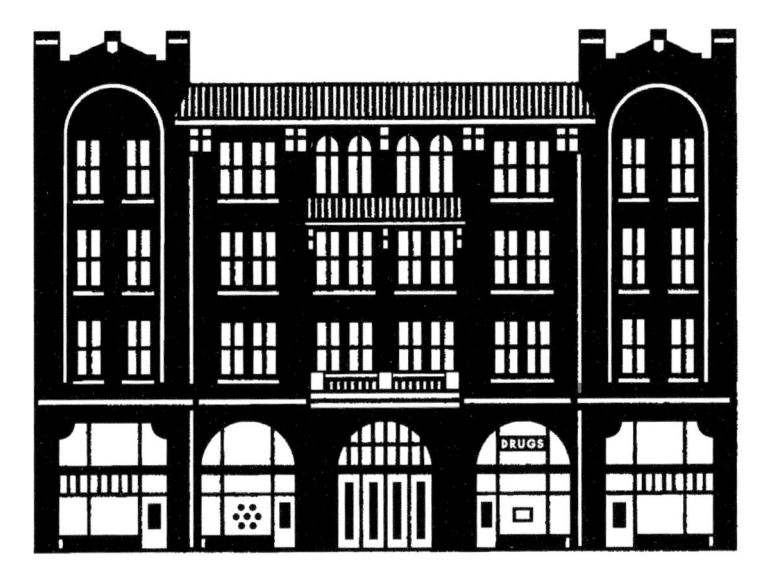

**Marquis Hotel** 1928-1988. Designed by Ernest Thomas Brown.

The architect Brown designed this four-storey hotel with some Spanish-castle details, including sections of sloped tile roof and faux battlements. But it was not named after some Spanish noble; its namesake was Marquis wheat, a quick-maturing variety whose introduction improved the fortunes of local growers. The Lethbridge Community Hotel Association developed the building in 1928 as a community hotel, raising $100 shares from local citizens. It also housed the Marquis Coffee Shop and Marquis Flower Shop. Nearby, the Marquis Beauty Shop and Marquis Taxi were separate businesses, all paying tribute to grain. **4th Avenue South and 7th Street South; now a Royal Bank.**

# KELOWNA, British Columbia

The name Kelowna speaks to the history of the Syilx Okanagan on the land; it comes (distantly) from their word for a male grizzly bear. European settlement didn't really begin here until 1859, and when Kelowna became a city in 1905 it had only six hundred people. The CP Rail didn't arrive until 1925. Architecturally, this is a twentieth-century city, and its buildings are the fruit of a time when houses could rise quickly for a gold rush and a great public building could come and go within two generations.

---

## Stocks Meadow Commune 1970s-2020

Reverend Phillip Stocks left Belgium in 1914 to find a peaceful place far from the battlefields of Europe. Fifty years later, his family had left his chosen site abandoned, though the place kept their name, and a new group arrived here to go back to the land. They built new cabins using materials salvaged from demolition sites. It was an entire compound of Stewart Brand–influenced hippie architecture, with one house shaped like a teepee and another apparently made of cob (clay, straw, and sand). About thirty people, parents and their children, lived here at the high point. There was a playground and solstice parties. Eventually the community dwindled to a few people, and a new owner bought the land, destroying what the Stocks Meadow group had built.

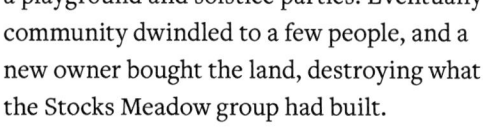

**Address unknown.**

**Old Post Office** 1937-1973. Designed by Robert Lyon.

Canada didn't build much during the Depression, but Kelowna did construct this remarkable post office. It was a bold work of art deco, in which the pilasters of the facade dissolved toward the sky in a forest of stone arrows. Lyon, the architect, was a Scot who had emigrated to Vancouver, worked for the BC Electric Railway, and then settled in Penticton, where he designed the municipal hall and became mayor. **Bernard Avenue and Ellis Street; now a bank branch and offices.**

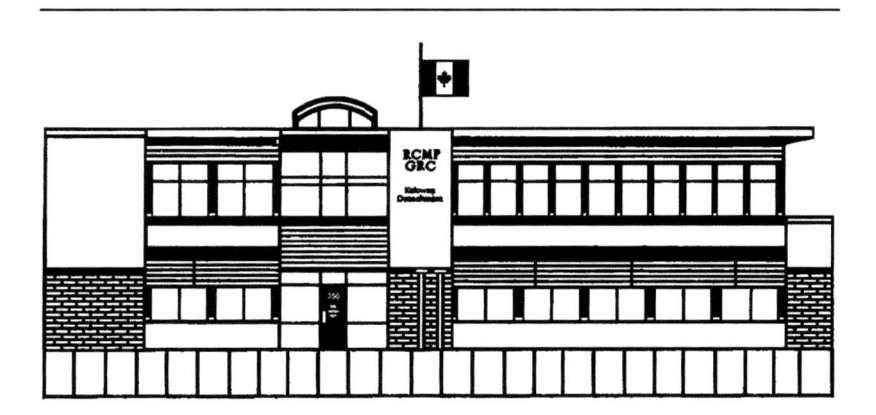

---

**Kelowna RCMP Detachment Building** 1962-2018

This station in the centre of town showed a clear Prairie Style influence. In 2017, the RCMP moved to a new building out on Richter Street, and the old one was used to hold men accused in a high-profile gang killing. With that last piece of business completed, the structure was demolished and is now being redeveloped as apartments, retail, and a civic plaza. **350 Doyle Avenue.**

# VANCOUVER, British Columbia

This is an exceptionally green and fertile region, and the Coast Salish Peoples found it a rich place to fish, grow, and live. Settlers took a different approach to the natural bounty: the colonial city grew up on panning for gold and cutting down trees. Railways came just after the city was incorporated, and the town grew from one thousand people in 1881 to one hundred thousand in 1911. This kicked off a dramatic twentieth century in which the wood from local forests created a city of comfortable houses, industry, and a bustling business district. Even in this young city, some meaningful places, particularly those associated with marginalized communities, have disappeared.

## Vie's Chicken and Steak House 1940s-1979

In the main floor of an old house on Union Street, with blue walls and red and yellow ceilings, Vie and Bob Moore ran a restaurant that welcomed everyone. This block, Hogan's Alley, was the centre of the city's Black community: it was near the railway station where many of the community's men worked as porters, and a rare place in the city where Black residents were welcome. Louis Armstrong found his way here when in town, and one of Vie's cooks, Nora Hendrix, would get visits from her grandson Jimi, who lived in her home for a time. Much of the Hogan's Alley neighbourhood was demolished for the construction of the Dunsmuir and Georgia Viaducts in the late 1960s. **209 Union Street.**

**Market Hall** 1890-1958. Designed by C.O. Wickenden.

With gingerbread-trimmed corner turrets and a porch with curved balusters, this was a very Victorian place of commerce. Yet it took on greater civic importance when it served as Vancouver's city hall from 1898 to 1929 (losing some of its trim in later years). After that, the hall served as an annex for the Carnegie Library next door. **425 Main Street; now a mixed-use building.**

---

**Mandarin Garden** 1918-1952. Designed by E. E. Blackmore.

By the 1910s, Vancouver had eclipsed Victoria to house the biggest Chinese community and the biggest Chinatown in Canada—a place to live, socialize, and organize. This building, designed for Chinese-Canadian owners by a local architect, first housed a grocery store, candy shop, and restaurant. By 1936 the building housed Mandarin Garden, a cabaret and restaurant serving both chow mein and Kraft-cheese sandwiches. It was levelled to make way for an extension of Columbia Street, during Vancouver's 1960s flirtation with highways.
**98 East Pender Street.**

**British Columbia**

**Stuart Building** 1910-1982. Designed by Henry B. Watson.

A wooden Edwardian apartment building that made it through the modern rebuilding of the West End. Lumber mill owner W.W. Stuart built it for $300, probably using his own products. In later years it housed a bike rental shop and art gallery but was most notable as an Edwardian survivor, its turret a rare trace of an earlier generation of buildings. **West Georgia and Chilco Streets; now a mixed-use building.**

---

**Birks Building** 1913-1974
Designed by Somervell & Putnam.

The Montréal-based jeweller often used architecture to give its shops cachet. Here, that meant an eleven-storey office building with a terracotta facade and a gracefully curved corner. The public was shocked when it came down, and it inspired a mock funeral in 1974, galvanizing the local preservation movement. Its clock survives at Granville and Hastings. **718 Granville Street; now Scotia Tower and a London Drugs.**

**British Columbia**

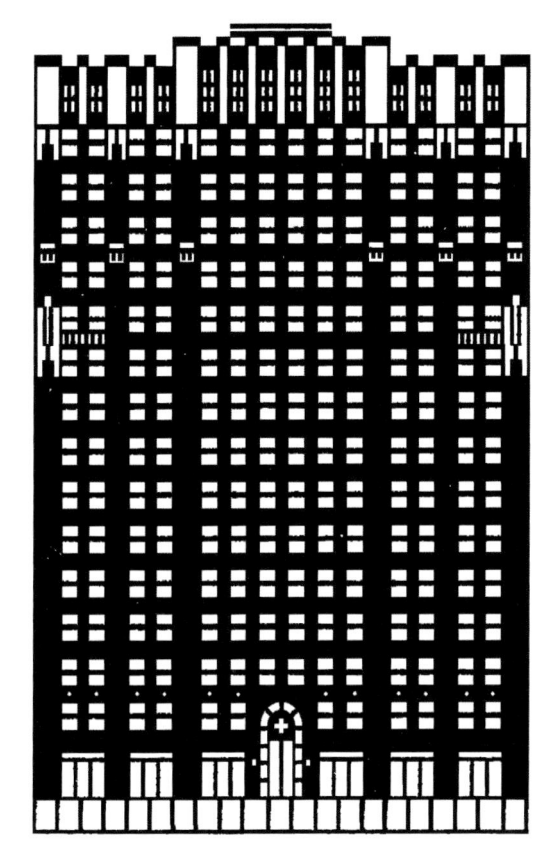

**Georgia Medical-Dental Building** 1928-1989
Designed by McCarter & Nairne.

Vancouver's first art deco skyscraper stood on the city's first skyscraper block, which included the old Hotel Vancouver. As its name suggested, this seventeen-storey tower was fitted out with medical convenience: it contained X-ray rooms and an operating theatre. The facades (by the same architects who designed the Marine Building) included three terracotta sculptures of nurses in First World War uniforms, looking out rather fearsomely from the corners of the tenth floor. Replicas of these sculptures were installed on Cathedral Place, which replaced this building. The originals were saved and installed at the UBC Technology Enterprise Facility.
**925 West Georgia Street; now Cathedral Place.**

## Vancouver Athletic Club
1906-1946

Craftsman-style cladding made it look like a house, but this club included a gym with a gallery for 1,600 people. One early manager was George Paris, a Black man who was both the heavyweight boxing champion of Western Canada and a professional jazz drummer. In 1909 Jack Johnson, who would become world heavyweight champion, fought an exhibition match here. Paris offered Johnson a place to stay after all local hotels turned him away, and Paris would become his trainer. **Dunsmuir and Beatty Streets; now 111 Dunsmuir.**

**The Orillia** 1903-1985. Designed by Parr & Fee.

Built for lumber baron William Tait, the Orillia resembled a row of Craftsman-style houses stacked on top of a row of storefronts. This architectural camouflage disguised the reality of a rooming house built at a time when rooming houses and hotels were related and, with their promise of life outside the family, widely distrusted by city leaders. The block allegedly housed a brothel and certainly housed a gay bar, known first as Twiggy's and later as Faces. **Now a mixed-use building at 605 Robson Street.**

**British Columbia**

**Union Station** 1917-1965. Designed by Fred Townley.

Around 1910, CN Rail and J.J. Hill's Great Northern Railway collaborated on a plan to fill in the eastern end of False Creek for rail yards. The two lines built competing stations next door to each other, in competing breeds of Edwardian classical pomp. The *Vancouver Sun* called the deal to fill in the flats "a rotten bad bargain," but it reshaped the city. The Great Northern eventually moved its service into the CNR station, closed its vacant building, and tore it down to save costs. **Station Street; now a parking lot.**

## Provincial Court House

1889-1914
Designed by Thomas Sorby and expanded by N.S. Hoffar.

Vancouver's first provincial courthouse lasted a brief twenty-four years. It grew with the city from a modest rusticated-stone structure to a larger domed and porticoed Palladian one. This, in turn, was replaced by a new courthouse (now the Vancouver Art Gallery). As for the old building, a newspaper letter-writer claimed it was "simply incommodious and inconvenient." A Conservative provincial government made plans to sell it for development. After the 1916 election, a new Liberal government gave it to the city for use as a war memorial.
**Now Victory Square.**

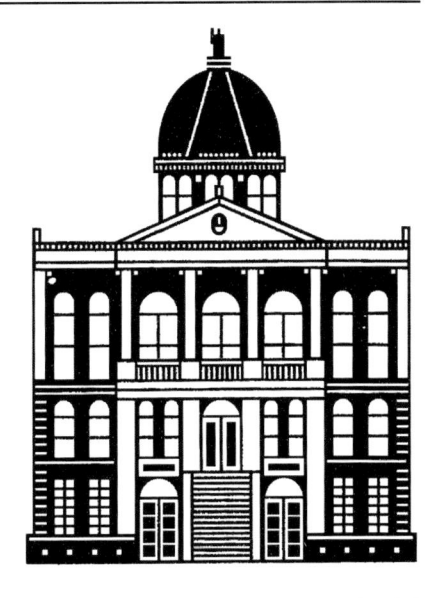

**British Columbia**

## Pantages Theatre

1908-2011

Designed by Edward Evans Blackmore.

The second in Alexander Pantages's famous chain of theatres, this 650-seater had an ornate interior with stone and scagliola. Charlie Chaplin and Houdini reportedly performed here. Later, it served as a movie house from the 1920s through 1994, by which time it was called the Sun Sing and was showing Chinese films. It sat empty for a decade, redevelopment plans never succeeding, until it was crumbling and was demolished. **150 East Hastings Street; now a mixed-use building.**

---

## Vancouver Opera House 1891-1961

Designed by John and Edward Hopkins; redesigned by E.W. Houghton.

The railways conducted many businesses besides rail travel. Canadian Pacific constructed the first Hotel Vancouver near its downtown station and ran this major performance house nearby, using it as a draw for passengers. In its early years, this was one of three "opera houses" in the city; later it was rebuilt and expanded by a vaudeville chain, and architect Houghton added Ottoman-style turrets. A later rebuild added office space, then came demolition and the Eaton Centre. **731 Granville Street; now Pacific Centre.**

**Second Hotel Vancouver** 1916–1949. Designed by Francis S. Swales.

During the 1910s, this Canadian Pacific hotel emerged in several phases as a massive Italianate pile ornamented with terracotta buffalo and moose; its tallest wing rose to sixteen storeys. By 1939, CP had teamed up with CN to complete the next (and current) Hotel Vancouver, which had stood half-built through much of the Depression. This seven-hundred-room predecessor served as a barracks during the Second World War. After the war, a veterans group commandeered it to house their comrades, which it did for two years. **West Georgia and Granville Streets; now Pacific Centre.**

**Ridge Theatre** 1950-2013
Designed by Kaplan & Sprachman.

The Ridge was a single-screen theatre that opened as a neighbourhood movie house (with *Henry V*, starring Laurence Olivier), and would go on to serve the Vancouver International Film Festival and as the city's leading rep cinema. Theatre specialists Kaplan & Sprachman's building politely concealed its bulk behind a row of shops. Its most visible aspect was a large neon sign, which now tops a condo and grocery store. **3131 Arbutus Street; now a mixed-use building.**

---

**Vancouver Art Gallery** 1931-1985. Designed by Sharp & Thompson.

The first home of the VAG showed its colours up front: the names of great painters were carved on a frieze on the front facade, and busts of Michelangelo and Leonardo marked the entrance. (Their gazes might have caught the gas station that stood next door.) A major expansion in the 1950s made room for a trove of Emily Carr works and replaced the facade with a modernist one. The building was demolished after the VAG moved to its current location. **1145 West Georgia Street; now Trump International Hotel and the Fortis BC Centre.**

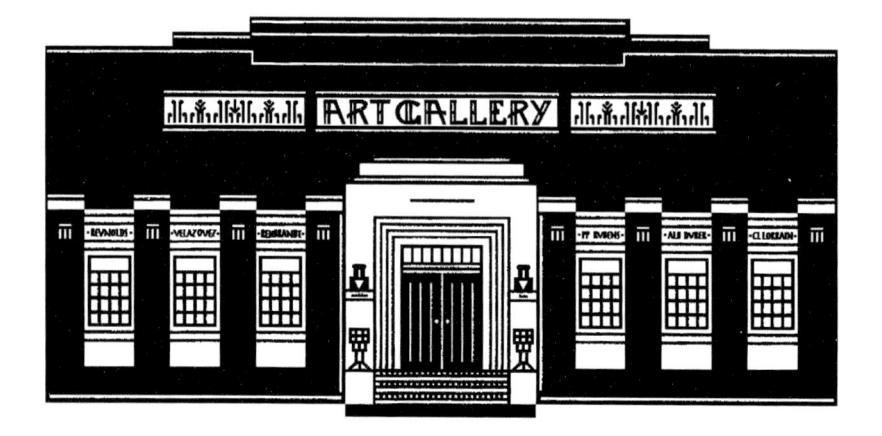

## Little Mountain 1954-2009
Designed by Sharp, Thompson, Berwick & Pratt and Semmens Simpson.

This was Vancouver's first modern social housing project, built to house returning veterans. Its 224 homes, in houses and walkup apartments, were scattered irregularly across a green fifteen-acre site. Both the unadorned architecture and the arrangement reflected trends in British and Scandinavian social housing. In 2007, the site was transferred from the federal government to the province, and BC Housing sold it to a developer. Much of the site remains empty, to the chagrin of former residents.
**Between 37th and 33rd Avenues & Main and Ontario Streets.**

## Majestic Theatre 1918-1967. Designed by B. Marcus Priteca.

Built as the second Pantages Theatre in Vancouver, this 1,800-seater was an active part of the vaudeville circuit, sometimes holding twelve hours of performances a day. Movie-palace pioneer Priteca designed it in the French Renaissance style, with an ornate white terracotta front, and the *Vancouver Sun* called it "one of the handsomest buildings of its kind on the Pacific coast." It would become known as the Beacon Theatre and shift to showing movies before being torn down for a parking lot. The Portland Hotel Society hired Arthur Erickson to design supportive housing on the site, which was completed in 2000.
**20 West Hastings Street; now the Portland Hotel building.**

British Columbia

## Electric House 1922-2017

Designed by Townley & Matheson.

A conservative house with radical systems, this building had nearly two hundred electrical outlets, an intercom, and closet lights that turned themselves on. It was a show house for a lobby group, the Electric Service League, which, according to an advertisement, "hope[d] to educate prospective homebuilders to the advantage of…electric conveniences." Townley & Matheson, who also designed the moderne Vancouver City Hall, dressed up this high-tech house in Tudor architecture that blended into upper-class Shaughnessy. **1550 West 29th Avenue; now a new house.**

---

## David Graham House 1963-2007

Designed by Arthur Erickson and Geoffrey Massey.

The views were remarkable, but this cliffside site was nearly impossible to build on. "The only solution that I could see was a multi-storey house set against the cliff like a ladder," Arthur Erickson would write later. "Its pleasure would be in the discoveries of the descent itself." Thus one of Canada's greatest architects fit the site with a "ladder" of glue-laminated wood beams delicately balanced above great viewfinding panes of glass. But by the time a local developer bought and wrecked it, this seminal work had been much altered and degraded. Building a masterpiece here was possible after all; preserving it was something else. **6999 Isleview Road, West Vancouver; now a new house.**

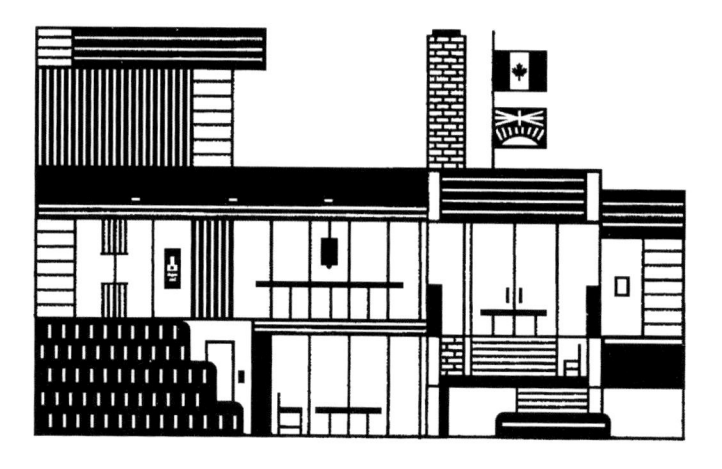

**British Columbia**

## VICTORIA, British Columbia

Vancouver Island in the mid-nineteenth century was among the most remote places in the British Empire. Victoria, settled in the 1840s, grew quickly in the next half century, initially under the control of the Hudson's Bay Company and on the trade of the British Royal Navy. Land was "purchased" from Indigenous groups in the area. Then, eureka: the 1858 Fraser River gold rush brought waves of prospectors, and those ready to sell to them and take their gold. Victoria became British Columbia's banking centre for many years, and its role as provincial capital brought both money and ambitious architects such as Francis Rattenbury. A huge building boom before the First World War remade the downtown. The late twentieth century was relatively gentle on the city's history, but early houses, important public buildings, and even skyscrapers have all gone down.

---

**Trounce House** 1859-1967. Designed by Thomas Trounce.

Architect, builder, councillor, mayor, and Masonic grandmaster, Thomas Trounce stood tall in nineteenth-century Victoria society. Originally from Cornwall, England, he chased gold in California and then British Columbia. His lasting success, though, was as architect of 350 buildings in the city, including those on Trounce Alley and this house for his own family. The house was named Tregew, after a Cornish village.
**436 Michigan Street;
now an apartment building.**

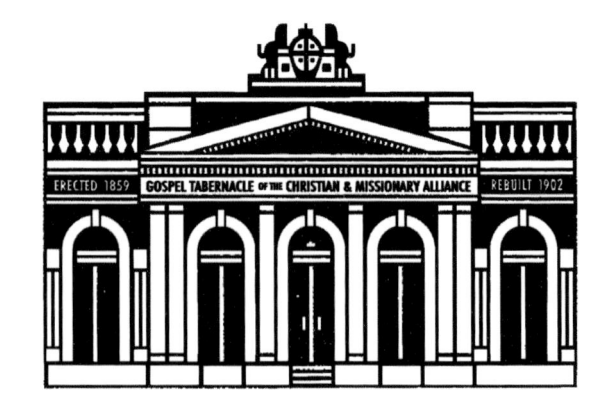

## Bank of British North America

1860-1949. Designed by Wright & Sanders, rebuilt 1902 by W.R. Wilson.

In its early days, Colonial Victoria hardly had enough commercial activity to keep a bank busy, and then suddenly, with the Fraser River gold rush, there was much gold to be stored, and two banks opened their doors, including this downtown branch of a colonial bank (the cornerstone was laid in 1859 and the building erected the following year). A 1902 reconstruction added appropriately classical flair to the place, including a six-columned portico. In later years this temple became a missionary church.

**571 Yates Street; now a parking garage.**

---

## Lucky Lager Brewery

1892-1983. Designed by Herman Steinmann.

Gold brought miners to Victoria, and miners brought a thirst. Victoria Brewing and Ice built this Richardsonian Romanesque complex. A local newspaper reported that "eighteen bricklayers, nineteen stonecutters, twenty laboring men, and twenty carpenters" were on the job. A tall tower allowed gravity to help the brewing process. The brewery survived Prohibition and became part of Lucky Lager in 1954. But even the largest independent brewers had little future. Labatt soon bought out Lucky and tore down the building in 1983 to move its breweries to the mainland.

**Discovery and Government Streets; now a strip mall.**

**British Columbia**

**Victoria Public Market** 1891-1962. Designed by John Teague.

In 1891, the City of Victoria destroyed a large part of its Chinatown, near city hall, to make way for a new public market structure. It featured a seventy-metre-long facade of arches, a large skylight, and space for sixty stalls. The place's strict regulations, however, made it unattractive to farmers. It housed instead a grab bag of tenants such as a portrait painter and the city morgue. Later uses included a fire hall and rail station. A 1960s revamp of the civic precinct saved city hall but demolished seventeen buildings, including the market. Preservationists protested for days; in the end, some of the market's brick went into constructing planting beds in Muirhead & Justice's new square. **Now Centennial Square.**

---

**Victoria High School** 1902-1953. Designed by Francis Rattenbury.

Western Canada's oldest public high school began with a log cabin in 1876. For its third home, Rattenbury designed this Collegiate Gothic building, which also housed the University of Victoria in its early days. Vic High moved on to its current site in 1914, and Rattenbury's double-gabled Gothic was demolished in 1953 for a modernist middle school.

**Fernwood Road and Yates Street; now Central Middle School.**

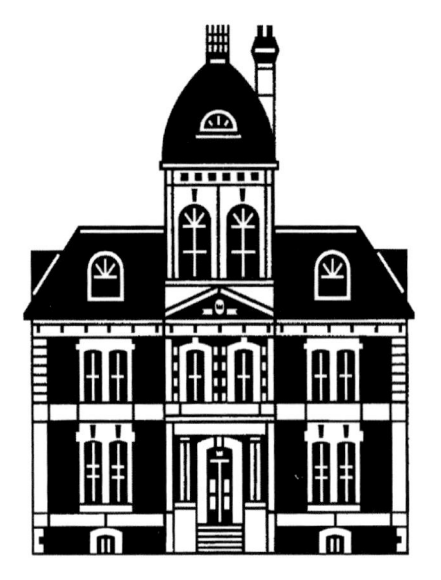

## Royal Jubilee Hospital

1890-1962. Designed by John Teague.

Home Hospital (later Royal Hospital) was founded in 1858, at the beginning of the gold rush. A new building was planned to be ready for Queen Victoria's jubilee in 1888. Teague, already the architect of Victoria's city hall, entered the hospital design competition, hiding his identity behind the motto "Work and Win." He did, with a Second Empire design. In 1893, the hospital proved invaluable in a smallpox epidemic. It wouldn't be the last, and the hospital was expanded several times before the original wing was destroyed. Teague would be mayor in 1894-95. **Fort Street and Richmond Road.**

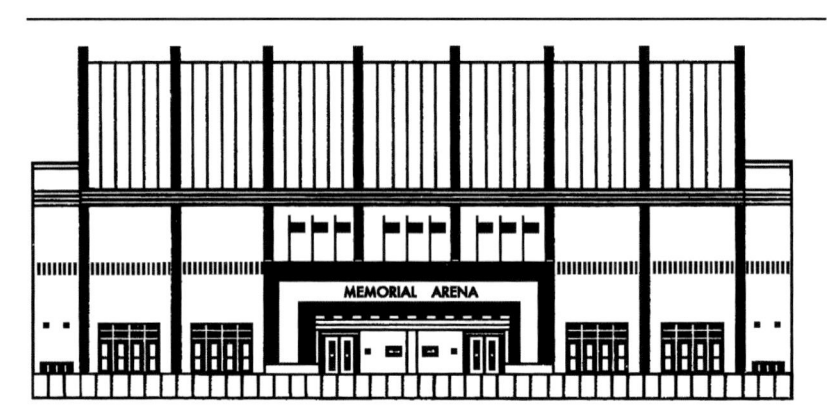

## Victoria Memorial Arena 1949-2003

Designed by David Frame, Douglas James, & Hubert Savage.

Canada's first arena with an all-concrete structure, the "Barn on Blanshard" was conceived as a Second World War memorial. Its construction was a four-year war in itself, with cost escalations, design changes, and errors. Locals stole lumber from the site; the new boiler didn't fit though the boiler-room door. Nevertheless, its barrel roof housed half a century of junior hockey, lacrosse, Duke Ellington, and Nickelback. **1925 Blanshard Street; now Save-on-Foods Memorial Centre.**

## Haida Theatre 1914-1993
Designed by Harold Ferree.

Once, this structure was a meeting hall for the Ancient Order of United Workmen. An ornate stone base disappeared after it became the Princess Theatre; later it became a cinema, acquired a marquee and canopy, went through two name changes, and wound up modernized as the Haida. Then, empty and crumbling, it met its end. **808 Yates Street; now The Atrium.**

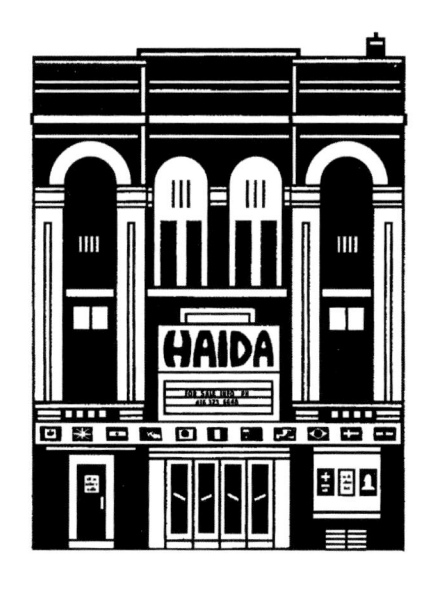

## BC Permanent Loan Building 1913-1968
Designed by H.S. Griffith.

The first building in Victoria to reach ten storeys, this was the tallest building in the city for half a century. Griffith's design was sober Edwardian classical, with a segmented arch over the main entrance modestly signaling the wealth of the Permanent. The tower was eventually replaced by another, shorter one, which remains. **1405 Douglas Street; now a TD tower.**

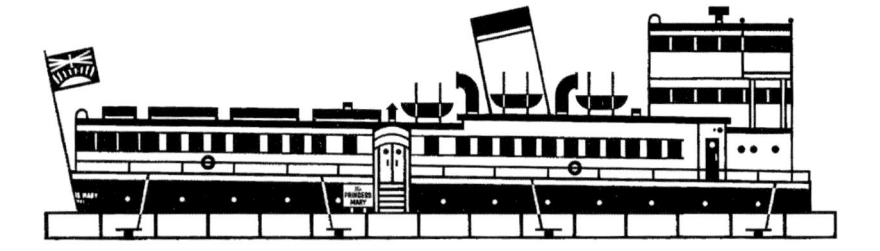

## The Princess Mary 1910-2011

The *Princess Mary* was built for the CPR in 1911, and spent forty years as a ferry in CP's British Columbia coastal service, travelling as far as Alaska. When it was mothballed, the hull was sunk, but its superstructure was beached and repurposed as a restaurant—a shell of a steamship that served seafood by the seashore. **358 Harbour Road; now the Dockside Green mixed-use project.**

---

## Canadian Pacific Steamship Terminal 1905-1924
Designed by Francis Rattenbury.

The CPR went into the ferry business here in 1901; its flagship offered service from Victoria to Vancouver in just four hours. To design a terminal it hired Rattenbury, who had designed the nearby Parliament Buildings and would soon design the Empress Hotel. Within a generation, the number of ferrygoers swamped the terminal, and CPR asked Rattenbury to design its replacement, which still stands.
**470 Belleville Street.**

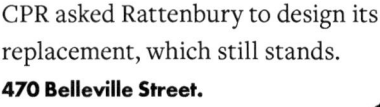

## The Poplars
1870s-1951
Designed by John Teague.

David Spencer started in business in Victoria with a bookstore; it grew to a block-long department store and eight others. He hired the prominent architect Teague for a series of buildings that included this large house, named for a row of poplars that protected it from winter winds. Spencer moved in his later years to a different house on Moss Street, which now houses the Art Gallery of Greater Victoria. **603 Belleville Street; now the Royal British Columbia Museum.**

## Campbell Building 1912-1976
Designed by Thomas Hooper.

Druggist Duncan Campbell built this seven-storey skyscraper when Douglas was the city's unquestioned main street. The Gladding-McBean Company shipped 117 tons of terra-cotta for the building's facades and created animal heads to decorate them. The architectural drawings showed moose, but Mr. Campbell's building wound up with camels. One head remains on display at a local mall. **1029 Douglas Street; now a Royal Bank.**

**Mount Baker Hotel** 1893-1902. Designed by Alfred Bodley and Samuel Maclure.

The Canadian Settlers Co. built this hotel on eleven acres of waterfront land, with fifty-seven rooms and eight bathrooms. At the time, Oak Bay was a place to get away from Victoria. The hotel burned in 1902, and a new Oak Bay Hotel was built on a different site; this too disappeared as Oak Bay evolved into a suburb. **Now Oak Bay Marina.**

---

### Chinese Masonic Hall 1900-1964

Victoria's first substantial number of Chinese immigrants came with the gold rush in the late 1850s. Many were members of mutual-aid societies, known in English (through an approximate translation) as Chinese Freemasons. The Chee Kung Tong was one such society. Established in 1876, it built this hall in 1900. The ornamented balcony was its only obvious reference to Chinese architecture. Dr. Sun-Yat Sen reportedly visited the site, and his statue stands there today. **617 Fisgard Street; now Centennial Square.**

**British Columbia**

## Oak Bay Boathouse 1893-1962

First built next to the Mount Baker Hotel at the end of Orchard Avenue, this boathouse survived when the hotel burned to the ground. It went on its own voyage, floated to a new site on Turkey Head in 1915. In 1925, a yacht was built inside that was too big to remove, so a beam of the boathouse had to be cut. The walls were never straight after that. **Beach Drive; now Oak Bay Marina.**

---

## Crystal Palace 1891-1907. Designed by C.J. Soule.

Like many of Canada's permanent exhibition halls built in the late nineteenth century, this was named after the Crystal Palace at the London Great Exhibition of 1851. The BC Agricultural Association's palace was a spectacular example: cross-shaped from above, it featured tall, round-headed ranks of windows pushing through intensely patterned wooden cladding and an ornate turret. It was a cathedral for cattle and commerce.
**Willows Fairgrounds; now the Carnarvon Park neighbourhood.**

**British Columbia**

### Federal Immigration Detention Hospital 1909-1978
Designed by William Henderson.

After decades of immigration to Victoria with few facilities, the federal government constructed this new building in 1909. It was both hospital and detention centre; the roles of immigration agent and medical doctor were interwoven. Policy was frankly racist, and the new hospital was racially segregated at first, designed to accommodate "ninety-six Hindus, thirty-six women, twenty-four Chinese, forty-eight Japanese, and sixteen others," as a contemporary source put it. Despite its attractive architecture and grounds, the building's dark history gave it an uncomfortable place in local history. It stood empty from 1958 to its demolition in 1978. **Dallas Road & Ontario Street; now a Canadian Coast Guard facility.**

# GLOSSARY

**art deco:** a style of design popularized by the 1925 Paris Exposition of Decorative Arts, characterized in architecture by strong geometric forms and colourful, often abstract ornament.

**art moderne:** a 1930s and 1940s descendant of art deco, with flat surfaces and minimal ornament. Strong horizontal lines evoked speeding cars and airplanes.

**Arts and Crafts:** a nineteenth-century English movement that emphasized traditional craft in architecture and household goods. Its founders were opposed to the social and cultural effects of the Industrial Revolution and to the perceived excess of ornament in Victorian architecture.

**ashlar:** stone with smooth-cut edges and rough-cut faces, laid horizontally, usually at the base of a building.

**bay:** a vertical division of a building.

**brick:** a unit of clay baked in a kiln, used for both structural and decorative purposes.

**brutalism:** a style of modernism characterized by a roughness or honesty in materials, particularly concrete. (The name arguably descends from the French phrase "béton brut," or "raw concrete.") Popular in Canadian institutional and apartment buildings of the late 1960s and 1970s.

**Chicago Style** or **Commercial Style:** tall commercial or industrial buildings with large windows, steel structures, and masonry facades with applied ornament. Pioneered in Chicago in the 1880s.

**cladding:** the outer, visible layer of materials on a building.

**column:** a basic element of classical architecture, a vertical support consisting of base, shaft, and capital.

**concrete:** an artificial material made from cement, sand, gravel, and water, shaped within (usually wooden) forms and reinforced with steel bars.

**corbel:** an element of stone or brick protruding from a wall and larger at the top, often supporting an element above. When in brick, each layer of brick protrudes above the layer below it.

**curtain wall:** a system of glass, with no structural function, that forms part or all of a building's cladding.

**entablature:** in classical architecture, the parts of the roof supported by the columns, generally consisting of architrave, frieze, and cornice.

**Georgian:** architecture shaped by the restrained British neoclassicism of the Georgian period (1714-1830), which draws on Italian Renaissance precedents, including Palladio.

**Gothic** and **Gothic Revival:** a popular style of the nineteenth and early twentieth centuries, especially for churches and academic buildings, that imitated European architecture of the Middle Ages.

**International Style:** a genre of modernist architecture characterized by open floor plans, horizontal strip windows, and unornamented, often white exterior surfaces.

**mansard:** a steep roof, associated with Paris and the seventeenth-century architect Francois Mansart and often imitated in the nineteenth century.

**modernist:** the constellation of architectural styles that originated in Europe around 1900 and took root in Canada later, often characterized by functionalism, a lack of ornament, and freely composed facades.

**neoclassical:** revivals of classical architecture, either Greek or Roman, which in Canada were often associated with institutional buildings and banks.

**neo-Tudor:** a nineteenth-century revival of sixteenth-century English architecture, characterized by steeply gabled roofs, the use of stucco, mullioned windows, and exposed (sometimes decorative) timber structure.

**Palladian:** after the sixteenth-century Andrea Palladio, known for his harmoniously designed Renaissance villas. A Palladian window is an arched window flanked by columns and flat-topped windows.

**picturesque:** irregular, asymmetric architecture; defined by nineteenth-century British aesthetics in opposition to the symmetry and order of classicism.

**portico:** a large porch in classical architecture.

**postmodernism:** an architectural movement that called for a playful and self-conscious use of historical forms and details. Widely influential, often in diluted form, in the 1970s and 1980s.

**Queen Anne:** a revivalist style popular after 1880 that fuses classical detail with picturesque asymmetry and copious decoration.

**Richardsonian Romanesque:** a revivalist style initiated by the American architect H.H. Richardson in the 1880s, often seen in Ontario around 1900; it combines Romanesque arches and stonework with irregular composition and eclectic ornament.

**Romanesque:** early-medieval European architecture characterized by symmetry and round arches, revived in the nineteenth century.

**Second Empire:** the style of Napoleon III's reign (1852-1870), popular in Canada in the 1870s and 1880s for institutional buildings and grand houses. Characterized by mansard roofs, symmetrical composition, and copious decoration.

**stripped classical:** a style that combined classically composed, symmetrical facades with a lack of ornament characteristic of modernism. Popular in English Canada from the 1930s to the 1950s with institutions such as banks and insurance companies.

**terracotta:** literally "cooked earth." Baked clay, used often for architectural cladding with a variety of coloured glazes.

**Victorian:** of the Victorian era (1837-1901), which in Canada encompassed a variety of revivalist architectural styles including Gothic Revival and Queen Anne.

**Vitrolite:** a brand name that also refers to a type of material. Coloured, structural glass popular on shop fronts from the 1930s through the 1950s.

# ACKNOWLEDGEMENTS

I wish I could draw these acknowledgements instead of writing them. If *305 Lost Buildings of Canada* is a dual-pyramid, Alex and I are on top of each structure. What lies inside his pyramid is a mystery to me—all I know is that words come out of it, and they describe my work better than I can.

The inside of my pyramid is clearly visible, though. Layer after layer has been laid down by the appreciated labour of others. At the bottom are the architects who built these buildings, and they're working decades ago and immediately below the people who (accidentally or intentionally) sketched, photographed, and described the buildings in print. Above them? The people (or natural forces) who knocked the buildings down. Above them? The people who took those sketches, photographs, and descriptions and put them online for myself, my thorough assistants (Zinta Avens Auzins and Amery Sandford) to find and be excited by and sort through. I've made mistakes and strange choices along the way, but these other people and forces have been essential to the construction of the pyramid.

I would especially like to thank agent Rob Firing, everyone at Goose Lane Editions, and everyone who bought a "Lost Buildings" print before the book was even conceived—your time and enthusiasm have kept the project rolling, far after I thought it'd be over. **— RB**

Thanks to Goose Lane and to Rob Firing. To Jocelyn Squires, for her research and counsel. To the following for their valuable assistance: George Baird, Bernard Flaman, Robert Hill, John Leroux, Shawn Micallef, Mark Osbaldeston, Josh Traptow, and Adele Weder, and to those I've overlooked. To the many historians on whose work I relied, especially Harold Kalman and Robert Hill. To the public libraries of Toronto, Hamilton, Montréal, Halifax, Regina, and St. John's, among others. Finally, and always, to Liv Mendelsohn. **— AB**

# THE AUTHORS

**Raymond Biesinger**, a Montréal illustrator originally from Edmonton, has spent a great deal of time touring the country while paying special attention to the built environment. His curious mix of geometric minimalism and detailed maximalism was first applied to architecture in his 2012-2016 *Canadian Cities* series of historically set urban landscape silkscreened prints. This series led to the *Lost Buildings of Canada* series, the inspiration behind *305 Lost Buildings of Canada*. A self-taught artist, Biesinger has been a part of more than a thousand illustration assignments on five continents since 2005. His work has appeared in numerous publications including *Billboard*, the *Economist*, the *Globe and Mail*, the *Guardian*, the *New Yorker*, and the *Walrus*.

**Alex Bozikovic** is the architecture critic for the *Globe and Mail*. He is co-author of *Toronto Architecture: A City Guide* with Patricia McHugh and *House Divided: How the Missing Middle Will Solve Toronto's Affordability Crisis* with Cheryl Case and John Lorinc. Bozikovic has also written for *Azure*, *Dwell*, *Icon*, and *Metropolis*. He won the 2019 President's Medal for Media in Architecture from the Royal Architectural Institute of Canada for his journalism. He lives in Toronto.